J Reaching ESUS

FIVE STEPS TO THE *fullness* OF LIFE

(Revised edition)

DAVID M. KNIGHT

Immersed in Christ
PUBLICATIONS

Second edition published as **Reaching Jesus, Five Steps to the Fullness of Life (Revised Edition)**
978-1-7327443-0-1
by *Immersed in Christ* 2095 Exeter Road, Suite 80–110
Germantown TN 38138
www.immersedinchrist.org

Cover design and book production by Adept Content Solutions

Back cover photo by Karen Pulmer Focht

Printed in the United States of America by C-M Books
(Cushing-Malloy, Inc.) 1350 N. Main, Ann Arbor, MI 48104.

CONTENTS

The "WIT" Prayer

Jesus, I give you my body.

Live this day with me.
Live this day in me.
Live this day through me.

Let me
Think with your thoughts, and
Speak with your words, and
Act as your body on earth.

WHY THIS BOOK?

The Essentials They May
Not Have Taught Us

In his 2018 letter, *Rejoice and Be Glad: On the Call to Holiness in Today's World,* Pope Francis is calling the whole Church "to be saints and not to settle for a bland and mediocre existence."

Jesus said he came that we might "have life and have it to the full" (John 10:10). That is what Christianity is: "life to the full."

Is that the way you experience it? Were you taught Christianity as a "mystery" that invites "endless discovery?" Has Paul's prayer been answered in you?

> I pray that you may have the power to comprehend, with all the saints, what is the breadth and length and height and depth, and to know the love of Christ that surpasses knowledge, so that you may be filled with all the fullness of God. (Ephesians 3:18)

Were you taught you are divine? That at Baptism you became, not just a Christian, but *Christ himself?* That is the teaching of the *Catechism of the Catholic Church,* quoting Saint Augustine:

> Let us rejoice then and give thanks that we have become not only Christians, but Christ himself. Do you understand and grasp, brethren, God's grace toward us? Marvel and rejoice: we have become Christ. (*No.* 795, from *In Jo. ev,* 21, 8)

Do you understand the mystery of your being? The wonder of what you are? Do you get out of bed every morning to let the infinite power of God act *with you* and *in you* and *through you* to give life to the world?

Are you a disciple of Jesus? Do you know that *disciple* does not mean "follower," but "student"? You are Christ's disciple only as long as you are *studying* his teachings. Are you doing that? Do you know the excitement of being enlightened by God? Do you experience being empowered by the Holy Spirit day after day to absorb the mind of God as it is revealed in his words? Do you know his heart?

Did anyone ever explain to you your "job description" as a Christian? It is contained in the words solemnly spoken to us at Baptism when we were anointed with chrism on the top of our heads:

> God the Father of our Lord Jesus Christ has freed you from sin, given you a new birth by water and the Holy Spirit, and welcomed you into his holy people. *He now anoints you with the chrism of salvation. As Christ was anointed Priest, Prophet, and King, so live always* as a member of his body, sharing everlasting life.

Christian life is a mission. These three words define it.

Pope Francis says, "You need to see the entirety of your life as a mission. Always ask the Spirit what Jesus expects from you in every decision you must make, so as to discern its place in the mission you have received" (*Rejoice and Be Glad*, no. 21).

Don't you find it incredible—mind-blowing—that God has chosen you to continue the mission of Jesus himself? You were solemnly anointed in Baptism by the Father, the Son, and the Holy Spirit to continue the messianic mission of Jesus as *Prophet, Priest,* and *King!* Do you know what that involves?

Do you know what a *prophet* is? How to go about being one in daily life? Do you know what is so exciting about it?

Your baptismal anointing made you a *priest in the Priest.* Do you think of yourself as a priest? Do you understand what that means? Are you aware of Jesus himself in you ministering to every person you deal with? Do you know how to make that a conscious experience?

Baptism made you a sharer in the *kingship* of Christ. Jesus has made you his *steward,* responsible for bringing about changes that will transform the world. Was it brought home to you that your "identification with Christ and his will involves a commitment to build with him a kingdom of love, justice and universal peace?" And that you "grow in holiness by committing yourself, body and soul, to give your best to this endeavor?" (*Rejoice and Be* Glad, no. 25)

There is more. Pope Francis said in *Rejoice and Be Glad,* "The first thing I would like to insist on is the *call to holiness.* It is my hope the whole Church will devote herself anew to promoting the *desire for holiness.* Let the grace of your Baptism bear fruit in a *path of holiness*" (10, 177, 15).

Call, desire, and path: For a *call* to awaken *desire,* it must offer a practical *path* to the goal. Were you shown a path to holiness?

If you were asked, "Can you show me the way to get holy?" could you instantly lay out a systematic plan for growing into the "fullness of the Christian life" to which the bishops at Vatican Council II said, "every believer is called"? They called it the "perfection of love" (*The Church,* 40, *Ecumenism,* 4).

Francis says, "The important thing is that each believer discern his or her own path, bring out the very best of themselves, the most personal gifts that God has placed in their hearts" (*Rejoice and Be Glad,* 11). But he insists on certain elements that must be common to every path. This book includes them all.

Business people say, "To fail to plan is to plan to fail." If you are looking for a plan, for a path blazed by saints and followed by Christians for centuries—sometimes without clearly recognizing the steps they were taking—that is what this book provides. It identifies five stages of the journey by five objectives to aim at. It translates the steps into five choices. Everything is clear, concrete, and surprisingly easy—to begin with.

Reaching Jesus was originally published in 1998. Since then it has been translated into French, Italian, and Arabic, and republished in Spanish, Polish, Korean, and Indonesian. So many individuals—and groups using the workbook—have read and discussed it since then that we feel a new, revised edition is desirable.

As you read, may the Father draw you. May Jesus, the Light of Life, teach you. And may the Holy Spirit—the Sanctifier—move your mind, your will, and your heart to grow to the "perfection of love!"

WHAT IT'S ABOUT

Five Choices

This book is about five steps—five words of response, five choices—that are essential to the decision to follow Jesus Christ. They are the five basic objectives we have to aim at in order to live authentically the divine life Jesus came to give: the life of grace. These five commitments are the loadbearing elements in a whole, an integral Christian life. They structure the total gift of ourselves in love.

Everyone desires "life to the full"—a full life, a meaningful life, a productive life, a happy life. However we understand and define these words, they are what our hearts desire.

Jesus of Nazareth defined himself as being both the fullness of life and the way to experience it. "I am the Way, and the Truth, and the Life." His reason for coming into the world was that we might "have life and have it to the full" (John 10:10; 14:6).

For two thousand years, Christians have proclaimed Jesus to be the "Christ"—the "Anointed One." But for each one of us individually, those two thousand years of communal belief are not as important as the one moment in our life when we make the decision to accept Jesus personally as the Savior of our own existence on earth and to base our lives on interaction with him.

The decision whether or not to believe that relationship with Jesus Christ is the way to the fullness of life we desire is the most important decision we will ever make, because it sets the course of our lives.

To believe that means to take it seriously. To just affirm in words that Jesus is the Savior of the world or to accept him as such intellectually is not functional belief. If we really believe we can find the fullness of life in relationship with Jesus, we will direct our whole life toward developing that relationship. We will interact with him in ways that let us discover who he is, understand what he teaches, embody his truth in our lifestyle, experience it in our relationships with others, and use it to transform the world.

Actually, this is not a single moment of decision; it is a recurring moment, a decision made and persevered in, a commitment. And commitments are the most important acts of our life. Commitments give shape to our souls.

Every decision, every free choice, is a moment of self-determination. Our free choices create us as the persons we will be for all eternity. In free choices we experience most deeply what it is to be human, to be like God. Every free choice is a "word" of self-creation: we say, "Let it be!" and it is. In free choices we choose to believe, to love, to hate, to live life to the full, or to turn away from life in its fullness. In these moments of freedom we create ourselves as believers, as lovers or haters, as people of hope or despair. Every free choice is a moment of freedom—the essence of humanness—lived. A commitment is a moment of freedom that endures.

Free choices are words that are spoken; commitments are words that are sung. In commitments we hold the note: the choice continues, and our moment of freedom is prolonged. Our commitments—the truths we choose to believe, the ideals we choose to embrace, the directions we choose to take, the goals we choose to pursue, the hopes we choose to live by—these are the enduring choices that give shape to our souls, make us the persons we are, determine the true meaning of our names.

Jesus Christ invites us to create ourselves, to shape our souls, by the response we make to him. This choice, this enduring decision, is the most important commitment of our lives. In fact, if we understand it as including all the particular commitments that follow from it and are included in it, it is the only commitment that counts. All other choices and commitments in life have no permanent significance, no enduring value, except insofar as, in one way or another, they are acts whose effects endure forever in the "eternal life" offered by Jesus Christ.

It is all about personal choice. Whether people respond to Jesus consciously, knowing his name, or whether, like the "wise men from the East" (Matthew 2:1) they respond to him under some other name by following a star through which God speaks to them, there is no other way that leads to life except the way that is Jesus. He, and he alone, is the Way, and the Truth, and the Life.

The purpose of this book is simply to mark the path so that those who choose to follow it will know where they are, understand what steps they have already taken, and what steps they need to take next in order to *reach Christ,* to arrive at that experienced union of mind and will and heart with him in which the fullness of life is found.

This book is about five words of response, five choices, five commitments. They are the five basic choices we have to make in order to live that "life to the full" Jesus came to give (John 10:10): the life of grace, divine life. These five commitments are required for a whole, an integral Christian life. They lead to the total gift of ourselves in love.

Each choice is a further step into life. But each choice also involves dying. Jesus said, "Those who want to save their life will lose it, and those who lose their life for my sake will find it" (Matthew 16:25). In each step we die a little more to ourselves in order to live a little more for God and others and love.

Pope Francis echoes Jesus:

At its core, holiness is experiencing, in union with Christ, the mysteries of his life. It consists in uniting ourselves to the Lord's death and resurrection in a unique and personal way, constantly dying and rising anew with him. (*Rejoice and Be Glad,* 20)

We come to holiness through repeated dying and rising. Read on to see what that involves.

STEP 1

THE CHOICE TO BE A CHRISTIAN

The first step toward "life to the full" is the choice to *make Jesus Christ as Savior an active participant in everything I do.*

That is what it means to be a *Christian*.

To do this I have to die to all trust in my ability to save any part of my life in this world without giving Jesus an active part in it.

This first step is one that will transform our whole life, but it is not difficult, vague, or complicated. It is a very simple—but deep—decision to do something very practical and very concrete.

It is to make a conscious act of faith that Jesus Christ is living within us. Then invite him to take part in our every thought, word, action, and decision.

You might pause to do this right now.

As Christians we believe that Jesus Christ is alive, that he is present to us all the time, that he sees our every action and hears our every word.

More than that, we believe he is present within us and that he lives in us by "grace," which means the gift of sharing in God's own infinite, divine life. By "grace" we share in the divine life of God, and Jesus shares in our human lives and in all our human actions.

"*Christ in you.*" St. Paul said these three words sum up the entire mystery he was sent to preach: "Christ in you." He added, "the hope of glory" (Colossians 1:27).

Whether we think about it or not and whether we explicitly choose it or not, as long as we are united to God by grace, Jesus has an active part in everything we do. There is not a word we speak, not a thought we have, or choice we make that Jesus does not influence—or try to influence, in the measure that we leave ourselves open to his action.

He doesn't just influence what we do. He acts *with us, in us,* and *through us,* expressing himself in our bodies, which are his body.

But Jesus will not violate our freedom. He will not force his influence on us. His union with us is a partnership: every graced choice and action has to be a joint decision. If we don't choose to cooperate with him, we put up an obstacle to his acting in partnership with us.

To live in partnership with Jesus, we need to make him an active participant in everything we do. That means *interacting with him consciously,* as much as we can, in every area and activity of our daily life.

Getting Practical: How Do We Do This?

To give Jesus an active part in all that we do, *awareness* is the key.

Pope Francis says:

Holiness consists in an habitual openness to the transcendent, expressed in prayer and adoration. The saints are distinguished by a spirit of prayer and a need for communion with God. They find an exclusive concern with this world to be narrow and stifling. They long for God, losing themselves in praise and contemplation of the Lord. (*Rejoice and Be Glad,* 147)

Jesus doesn't break in on our senses like other people do. He doesn't assail our eyes everywhere we look, like advertisements on a city street. He doesn't pound on our ears like TV commercials or a bystander's cell phone. If we want to be conscious of Jesus, we have to provide our own sensory reminders. And we can be creative about it.

First, we can program ourselves to remember. We can form the habit of reminding ourselves when we wake up each morning, "I want to give Jesus an active part in what I do today." Whenever we drive anywhere, we can think of how we might involve Jesus in what we are about to do—asking, for example, how he would do it. While driving home from work, we can think back on how conscious we were of him during the day and what difference it made. Before going to sleep, we can glance back over the whole day and ask the same question. If we keep doing this, we will grow into an abiding awareness of Jesus that will underlie our consciousness all day long.

If our culture has created an environment that ignores the presence of God, we can structure things into our personal environment that remind us of God.

Some people set their watches to beep every hour as a reminder to remember God's presence. Some put a picture on their desk or at their worksite. Others keep some symbol before their eyes whose meaning is known only to them. Some form the habit of thinking of Jesus every time they go through a door, start their car, or pick up the phone.

We can also use some gesture or body language that speaks to us but that no one else would notice: keeping our hand casually on our heart or our finger on our lips while we listen to someone speaking. And, noticeably or not, we can bow our head every time someone around us uses the name of God disrespectfully or insults another person. Whenever anyone's language shows a lack of appreciation for what is sacred—which includes every human person— we can consciously hear those words with Jesus, aware of how he feels about them.

Whenever a commercial comes on, we can remember Jesus and say a prayer—or comment to him about what we have just seen on the news or in a program.

Our senses belong to us. We can't control much of what other people force on our eyes or ears, but we can counterbalance the images, words, and sounds that are part of our environment by adding others of our own making. We can give Jesus equal time on the airwaves.

The Need to See the Need

What we are suggesting here sounds very simple. And it is. It is also very concrete and down-to-earth. There is no one who cannot do it.

So why is it that so many people don't?

The answer—for most, I think—is that they don't realize the need. Most people don't consult a doctor until they feel sick or ask for advice until they feel confused. And if Christians do not interact with Jesus as Savior all day, every day, it may be simply because they don't think such constant interaction with him is necessary. For many, "Jesus is Savior" may just mean Jesus has opened the gates of heaven for us, not that he wants to save everything we do, all day long.

So what does it mean to accept Jesus Christ authentically as Savior?

Before we can build our lives solidly on Jesus Christ as a foundation, we have to dig a hole. The deeper the hole, the stronger the foundation. This means we have to go deeply into ourselves and understand the need we have for him. We have to be deeply convinced that constant interaction with Jesus Christ is not an option, that seeking conscious, ongoing relationship with him is not an "extra" but the only way to save our lives here on earth from veering off into *destructiveness, distortion, mediocrity,* and *meaninglessness.*

If we think the choice to interact constantly with Jesus is just a choice to be "more," as in "more or less"—more Christian, more holy, more religious, as opposed to just "less perfect" in all of these—we don't understand the question. It is not a question of more or less, but of either-or.

The question is, "Do you believe Jesus Christ is the only one who can save your life from becoming what you really don't want it to be?" That means in your personal relationships, your family life, social life, and professional occupations. You need to understand this as an either-or: either make Jesus a real, operative participant in everything you do, or see your life "miss the mark" (the root meaning of "sin") and slide off into destructiveness, distortion, mediocrity, and meaninglessness.

The Root of the Problem: Original Sin

Why do we need to be so pessimistic? Aren't we all basically good people? Isn't our society founded on basically good principles and values? Isn't what we have learned from our religion enough? Aren't the Ten Commandments sufficient to keep us on course and living adequately good lives? Why do we have to relate consciously to Jesus and interact explicitly with him in everything we do?

The first answer is Original Sin. Yes, people are basically good. There is nothing flawed in the equipment God gave us to work with; there are no "factory defects" in our human natures. The sin of Adam did not jog God's creative hand and cause it to slip. So far as God's work is concerned, we are made perfectly according to specifications.

But beginning with the first sin ever committed on earth, the human environment changed. Because every human being born into the human race must grow up in a culture, in a formative society, when the human environment changed, the existential situation of every person born into this world was altered at the root.

We are social beings. The family, the society, the culture into which we are born radically influence our attitudes, values, and behavior. Before we are old enough to understand what we are doing or to make free choices, we are already being programmed by our milieu to feel, think, and act in particular ways, both good and bad. The world into which we are born shapes our initial attitudes, values, priorities, and patterns of behavior in ways too all-pervasive to analyze. Our environment has power over us, and no one—absolutely no one—is exempt from its influence.

This means that once sin came into the world, cultures began to influence everyone in bad ways as well as good. No one escapes. From the instant we begin to exist, we are already to some extent enslaved by culture, subject to the power of sin in the world.

This is the effect of Original Sin—and the cumulative effect of every free human choice that has injected falsehood or distortion into the environment, from the first sin to the most recent one. The world was not created bad; people were not created bad. But the environment into which all people are born was made and is being made now both good and bad by the free actions of individual human beings. And this is the environment that forms and shapes the fears and desires, the assumptions and prejudices, the emotions and perceptions, of every human being born into the world.

Because of the distortion of truth in the environment, our intellects will be darkened in what they understand. Because of the distortion of values our wills will be weakened by fears and misdirected desires. This is not a flaw in our nature as such; it is an existential characteristic of our being in the world we live in. It is something that defines human existence on earth. From the moment we are conceived in our mother's womb, we exist in solidarity with the human race and subject to its influence. That is what we are. In the world that actually is, some of that influence is going to be bad.

We are not saying the effects of Original Sin are something programmed into us by our interaction with the environment after we are born. They are part of our being, a characteristic of our existence, from the moment we begin to exist in our mother's womb. Because of what Original Sin has done to the environment, from the moment we exist we are already bound, doomed, to be influenced for both good and bad by our inevitable interaction with the infected environment of this world. Our essence, our nature is good. But we are existentially vulnerable. So we won't stay perfectly good for long.

This, in part at least, is the meaning of Original Sin. And this is why we are doomed by our culture to live and act in distorted and destructive ways—unless we are reformed, reshaped and recreated in our perceptions and judgments, in our attitudes and values, through interaction with Jesus Christ, the only true Light of the World. Only Jesus can show us without distortion the Way to live, and the Truth to live by. Only Jesus can lead us to Life. That is why he said, "I am the Way, and the Truth, and the Life. No one comes to the Father except through me" (John 14:6).

It is only through interaction with Jesus—constant, daily interaction with Jesus as Master of the Way and Teacher of Life—that we can gradually become free from the darkness and distortions of our culture, purify our values and desires, put aside the fears and priorities programmed into us by our society, and learn to live "life to the full." To seek this ongoing, constant interaction with Jesus as the Way, the Truth, and the Life is what it means to accept Jesus as Savior.

Jesus says to those who believe in him, "If you are truly my disciples, you will know the Truth, and the Truth will make you *free*" (see John 8:31).

What Does Good Mean for Christians?

There is another reason why we have to interact with Jesus in everything we do. It is because to act authentically as a Christian, it is not enough to live a good human life on ground level and keep out of sin. We have to act on the level of God.

Being "saved" doesn't mean just getting to heaven, any more than being "holy" means just keeping out of sin. Being saved means entering into life—and human life has varying degrees of fullness, ranging from just barely vegetating in a coma to making peak usage of all our human powers of body, intellect, and will. There is more to being alive than just not being dead.

And there is more to being saved than just living by God's laws. To be saved means to live by the *divine life* of God. We can be more or less saved, just as we can be more or less alive. Like the young man in the Gospel who had kept the commandments from childhood, we need to ask Jesus, "What is still missing in my life?" (Matthew 19:20)

All of us who are Christian recognize that we need Jesus to get to heaven, and most of us pray for his help against the temptations and sins we recognize as such.

But we do not pray for help against what we perceive as normal behavior. Once we have achieved a certain measure of control over our lives, enough to be accepted as mature, self-disciplined adults who live the way everyone expects us to live, we may not consciously feel any daily need for Jesus. We may think that what we are doing is good enough so long as we are not doing anything we recognize as positively wrong.

But are we really able to recognize what is wrong, given the distorted attitudes and values we grew up with? Did our ancestors recognize slavery as wrong? Segregation? What about Christians who burned one another at the stake over differences in belief? Some forced whole nations to their knees before the cross at sword point!

And if what we are doing is in fact good, how good is "good enough" for someone who shares in the life of God? Someone who is called to live on the level of God? Jesus called his disciples the "salt of the earth" and the "light of the world." Until we stand out as exceptional in the ordinary, daily actions of our life, we are not fully saved (Matthew 5:13). Pope Francis says Baptism calls us to a higher standard:

> To the extent that each Christian grows in holiness, he or she will bear greater fruit for our world . . . All you, the baptized, are called to take up your roles as salt of the earth and light of the world wherever you find yourselves. (*Rejoice and Be Glad,* 33)

We need to be awakened to see what we need to be saved from in order to be "salt and light." We can live for years not appreciating the real power of sin in our lives, not knowing what our crippling sins are, or even that we have any. Without deep interaction with Jesus Christ, we accept many evils as good, just because everyone else does.

Unless we measure ourselves constantly by the example and ideals of Jesus himself, we will unconsciously wind up accepting the common denominator of our society's standards as par for the course. To do this is to fall into the complacency of believing that even though we may not be perfect, we are, for all practical purposes, living perfectly good lives. We need Jesus as Savior in order to recognize the difference between darkness, semi-darkness, and light.

So before we can decide to make Jesus an active redeeming participant in our lives with any hope of persevering in this decision, we need to dig down into our hearts, go deep into self-knowledge, and lay a foundation of "*life-giving despair.*"

The emphasis is on "life-giving." But the despair is essential. We will have conscious, life-giving, inspiring hope in Jesus Christ only in the measure we see and feel very deeply that unless we give Jesus himself an active role in our lives, everything we do will tend to veer off into destructiveness, distortion, mediocrity, and meaninglessness.

Going Beneath the Surface

Some of us have lived long enough to know this by experience. We have seen marriages begin beautiful and end ugly. We have seen ourselves doing destructive things—to others and to ourselves—at work, in our social lives, as citizens, even as priests or laity engaged in ministry. It is just a fact that, without the involvement of Jesus in every area of our lives, anything we do is prone to slide off into destructiveness, distortion, mediocrity, or meaninglessness.

Where our lives are not destructive, we nonetheless recognize *distortion*. We gradually realize that many of the attitudes and viewpoints we absorbed from our culture are out of focus. We see that our family life, while not

screamingly destructive, is still not perfectly in balance.
We recognize a wrong set of priorities where we work, an
attitude in our social circle that is not right.

Even when our attitudes and values are not clearly
distorted, we sometimes sense a *mediocrity* in our lives that
tells us something must be wrong. Our marriage is good,
but not as good as it could be, not the fulfillment of our
dreams. Our work doesn't leave us satisfied at the end of the
day. Our social life is flat with superficiality. Even religion
doesn't always give us the peace, the joy we long for. We are
leading good lives but unsatisfying ones, "settling for a bland
and mediocre existence" (*Rejoice and Be Glad,* 1). We don't
taste the "fruit of the Holy Spirit" in everything we do: love,
joy and peace (see Galatians 5:22). We are not experiencing
that "life to the full" Jesus came to give (John 10:10).

Finally, there is the specter of *meaninglessness.* The
question that increasingly hangs over our heads in the
morning as we get up to begin another day is, "What is it
all about? Is it worth it? Is this what I want to do with my
life?" Even though we know our lives come from God and
lead to ultimate fulfillment in heaven, and even though at
times we experience ourselves doing wonderful things for
others or for God, we sometimes wonder doubtfully about
the long stretches in between.

We can't really appreciate Jesus as Savior—not as the
Savior he came to be—until we are deeply convinced, to
the very toes of our being, that unless we give Jesus Christ
an active part in everything we do, our lives here on this
earth cannot be saved from destructiveness and distortion,
from mediocrity and meaninglessness.

The Act of Life-Giving Despair

This is the act of life-giving despair. We despair of all
false messiahs, of anything and everything except Jesus

Christ that promises to save the meaning and value of
our lives on earth. False saviors are false gods. And to
trust in false gods is idolatry, a violation of the First
Commandment: "I am the Lord your God. You shall not
have other gods alongside of me" (see Exodus 20:2).

Before we can live that "life to the full" that Jesus came
to give (John 10:10), we have to look into our hearts and
give up all hope for a full and meaningful life that is based
on confidence in ourselves or in the way of living we
grew up with. We have to give up any security we find
in conformity to our culture. We have to stop relying for
fulfillment on the use of our talents and education, on
techniques and support groups, on the love of spouse and
children, on acceptance by other people, on rewarding
dedication to human service, on success.

To despair of finding satisfaction, peace, happiness, and
fulfillment through anything other than Jesus Christ is a
life-giving act of despair: an act that preserves us from false
saviors, false messiahs, false gods. It is the act that opens us
to radical hope in Jesus as Savior.

The Act of Faith in Jesus as Savior

Despair is not enough. What saves us is placing positive
faith and hope in Jesus Christ. We despair of false
messiahs in order to turn to Jesus with hope focused
uniquely on him. We acknowledge him with deep,
personal faith as the "only name under heaven given to
the human race by which we are to be saved" (see Acts
4:12). This is the act of totally life-giving hope. It is not
to be taken for granted.

Anyone who is Christian professes that Jesus is the
"Savior of the world." But for many this just means in

practice that we depend on Jesus to get us to heaven. How many Christians depend positively on Jesus for fulfillment in their family and social lives? In business and politics? How many teenagers take Jesus along when they date?

How many Christians show in real and observable ways that they believe interaction with Jesus can save every area of their life from destructiveness and distortion, mediocrity and meaninglessness? How many turn to him with this belief when a situation seems hopeless?

How many believe interaction with Jesus can save a marriage that is breaking up, change a nasty situation at work, or turn a bad relationship with someone into a good one? How many believe interacting with Jesus can change the way we think about ourselves? Or put our whole experience of life on a new, joyous and fulfilling level?

To believe this—and act on it—is to believe in Jesus as Savior. If we only believe that Jesus can get us to heaven, but not that he can transform our enjoyment of life on earth, then we only believe in him as the Savior of our souls, not as the Savior of all we are. It isn't enough. It doesn't do him justice. Jesus didn't come just to save our souls; he came to save us, to save everything about us, everything we do, everything we are.

He saves us by raising up everything we think and do to the level of God. To believe this—and to live it out by constantly asking Jesus Christ to act *with us, in us,* and *through us* in everything we do—is a basic foundation for living the divine life of God on earth.

It is also an ongoing mystical experience.

What Is a "Mystical Experience?"

The key to experience is *awareness.* An *experience* is something we are conscious of.

A *mystery* is defined as "a truth that invites endless exploration, endless new discovery." The only true mystery is God, because only God is infinite, "boundless." So we are having a "mystical experience" when we are conscious of being acted upon or interacting with the mystery of God.

Mystery is a fact of our being. Every one of us is living the mystery of the life of "grace," which is the gift of sharing in the divine life of God.

Every one of us is a mystery of the divine and the human combined in one life. We received human life when we were conceived in our mother's womb. But when we were conceived anew—when we died and came to life again "in Christ," in the tomb and womb of Baptism—our lives became a mystery of the divine and the human made one. Like the water that becomes indistinguishably one with the wine at Mass, we became a mystery of union with Jesus Christ in life and action. We became his body. Or more precisely, as St. Augustine said, we "became Christ."

Whether we understand it clearly or not, by the gift of *faith* we are sharing in God's own act of knowing. By the gift of *hope* we are setting our hearts on what God holds out to us and believing it is possible, sharing in God's intention to keep his promises. And by the gift of *love,* we are sharing in God's act of loving what God loves, desiring what God desires, and appreciating what God appreciates.

Being aware of this is a mystical experience. We are having a "mystical experience" whenever we do *consciously* what is divine.

The difference between those we call "mystics" and those we don't is a difference in awareness. We are all living the mystery of divine life, the mystery of union with Jesus in one body, the mystery of God's love poured out in our hearts with the gift of the Holy Spirit. But the "mystics" are more aware of it.

Should mystical experiences be everyday occurrences? If we are talking about the extraordinary experiences the mystic saints had—like the locutions, visions, raptures, and ecstasies St. Teresa of Avila writes about—the answer, of course, is "no." But if we are talking about the "ordinary mysticism" that consists in explicitly *experiencing* in some way the mystery of our graced being, becoming consciously aware of the divine action of God with and within us, then, yes, mystical experiences can be and should be our "daily bread."

The first step into consciously living "life to the full" is to cultivate the mystical experience of Jesus acting *with us, in us,* and *through us* in everything we do.

The Channels of Interaction

Just being aware of Jesus is not enough; we need to interact with him as we do with friends. And we can do this in several ways:

Rinky-dink Prayers: One way is to make constant use of what I call "rinky-dink" prayer. A rinky-dink prayer is a prayer for something that is not important enough to bother the Almighty about. When we make it, we become conscious that Jesus is our friend.

I discovered rinky-dink prayer one evening while putting a roof on a carport. I was pressing to finish before dark, and in my haste I kept dropping roofing tacks onto the driveway where I knew they would lie in wait for my car tires. I noticed that each time I dropped a tack and scrambled down the ladder to look for it, I would start to say a prayer: "Lord, help me find that tack!"

It irked me. I felt humiliated asking God for help to do what I was perfectly capable of doing myself. In an attempt to justify my irritation, I told myself, "If my best friend were president of the United States, I wouldn't call him up to fix a parking ticket!"

Then I thought: "No, but if he were visiting me and standing at the bottom of this ladder, the first thing I would do when I dropped a tack would be to yell down, "Hey, did you see where that tack went?"

I got the point. To let Jesus be a friend, we need to treat him as a friend instead of just as God. This is a way to grow into awareness of him as friend. Now I pray to him constantly, asking him to do anything I would ask a friend to do: "Lord, find me a parking place." "Show me a good restaurant." "Don't let me blow it during this phone call."

The point is, asking Jesus for things all day long keeps us conscious of him all day long—especially if we thank him for what he does.

Prayers of Petition: I don't have access to many powerful people. I can hardly get in to see my doctor sometimes, much less the movers and shakers of business and politics. But I have instant access to the Savior of the world: any time, any place. All of us do, as often as we want, for as long as we desire. There is no concern in our lives that we cannot present personally to Jesus Christ. And when we do, we are sure that we will be listened to with attention and with love. To go to Jesus with our petitions is a way of interacting with him that helps keep us aware of who he is for us and what he wants to be.

One of the early Jesuits, Saint Peter Faber, used to look out the window when he was traveling and pray for workers he saw in the fields, for children playing in the streets, for the occupants of a house that looked peaceful— or that did not. We can pray for drivers on the freeway who annoy us; for the people we deal with in business; for situations we see on the news; for our family, friends, and enemies. We can pray for better housing when we drive through poor neighborhoods, and when we drive through affluent neighborhoods, we can pray that all who live there will find peace in following the values and example of Jesus.

Pope Francis says,

> Let's not downplay prayer of petition. It is the expression of a heart that trusts in God and realizes that of itself it can do nothing. It calms our hearts and helps us persevere in hope. And, at the same time, it is an expression of our family concern for others, since we are able to embrace their lives, their deepest troubles and their loftiest dreams. (See *Rejoice and Be Glad,* 154)

That is what the "Prayer of the Faithful" is at Mass.

The Prayer of Consultation and Discernment: One of the most important ways of interacting with Jesus is to make him a part of every decision and action of our lives by consulting him beforehand.

We don't have to spend a great deal of time consulting him—unless we are making a very important decision that calls for a lot of prayerful reflection. But we should not make any decision without at least passing it by Jesus, asking him for guidance and asking ourselves what we believe he thinks about it. People who work as a team do this constantly. Partners consult each other. Married couples do. When we don't have time to talk over a decision, we at least ask ourselves mentally what the other would think of it. And we who are coworkers with Jesus Christ, who became his body at Baptism, who are consecrated and committed to bearing witness to him through every detail of our lifestyle, and are trying to advance the reign of God through everything we are involved in, should we not consult him before every decision we make? This is called the prayer of discernment.

Pope Francis tells us, "Discernment has become more necessary today, since contemporary life offers immense possibilities for action and distraction, and the world presents all of them as valid and good . . . Without the wisdom of discernment, we can easily become prey to every passing trend." (*Rejoice and Be Glad,* 165)

The Prayer Beyond Prayers: The most powerful way to make Jesus a part of everything we do is to participate weekly or daily in the mystery of the Mass. For some people daily Mass may be impossible because they are homebound or bound to inflexible schedules. But if all those who actually could were to offer themselves daily with Jesus at Mass for the redemption of the world, our churches would not be able to contain them. This is one of the greatest treasures of the Catholic Church, insufficiently exploited.

At Mass Jesus on the cross is made present in our space and time, offering himself as he did on Calvary. We who know this can be there, united to him, one with him as members of his body. We can offer him—and ourselves with him—as God's response and ours to all the sin and suffering we are so painfully aware of in the world we walk in each day. There is no better way to grow into consciousness of Jesus as Savior than to be united with him daily in the mystery of the act by which he saved and is saving the world.

The WIT Prayer: To make this first step a reality in your life, I would suggest one thing that is so easy and so life-transforming that everyone can do it. Form the habit of saying the "WIT prayer" every morning as soon as you wake up:

Jesus, I give you my body.

Live this day with me.
Live this day in me.
Live this day through me.

Let me
Think with your thoughts, and
Speak with your words, and
Act as your body on earth.

That is the WIT prayer: *W*-ith, *I*-n, *T*-hrough. Form the habit of saying it all day long, before everything you do: "*Lord, do this with me, do this in me, do this through me.*"

But saying the WIT prayer isn't going to happen just because you decide to do it. You will forget. That is normal. So, until it becomes a habit, you have to use something to remind you, a "gimmick."

What will work for you? Hanging something on your doorknob that reminds you every time you walk through the door? Programming your cell phone? Attaching something to your car keys? Tying a string on your steering wheel? Making WIT part of your password?

Saying the WIT prayer will transform your life. It will keep you conscious all day long that you are not alone, that Jesus is with you. And not only *with* you as the friend by your side, but *in* you, acting *with you, in you,* and *through you* in everything you say and do.

To be aware of this is to be aware of the mystery of your being as the divine body of Christ. To foster this awareness is to *make Jesus Christ a recognized participant in everything you do.*

That is to take a first step toward the fullness of life, toward being a conscious *Christian.*

QUESTIONS FOR REFLECTION
AND DISCUSSION

1. Is all this practical enough? Down to earth enough? Can I make a decision to put some of what I have read into practice? How will I start?

2. What areas of my life need to be saved from destructiveness? Distortion? Mediocrity? Meaninglessness?

3. What concrete actions could I take that would give Jesus an active part in these areas of my life? When, where, and how could I begin?

4. What effective reminder could I use to form the habit of saying the WIT prayer all day long?

STEP 2

THE CHOICE TO BE A DISCIPLE

The second step into the fullness of life is the choice to *lead a life characterized by reflection on the message of Jesus.*

That is what it means to be a *disciple*.

To do this I have to die to reliance on the goals and guidance of my culture.

The word *disciple* doesn't mean "follower." It means "student." To be a disciple of Jesus, one has to be a student of his, one studying under him here and now. How many Christians are doing that?

We ask the question, not to judge other people, but to understand why Christianity is not having more effect on the world today. How many Christians are thinking seriously about the teachings of Jesus? How many read the Bible regularly? How many are *students* of his?

There are many more today than there used to be. But we need to insist on the meaning of the word. If we are not sitting regularly at the feet of Jesus now, actively devoting ourselves in some way to absorbing his mind and heart, we are not disciples of Jesus Christ.

And we are missing out.

It is not "life to the full" just to believe in Jesus, observing all the laws and teachings we learned in grade school or high school religion classes—or even in college!—when we used to be disciples. The simple truth is, if we are not sitting at the feet of Jesus here and now, learning from him in some way now, we are not disciples.

We need to say it like it is. Since no one graduates from the school of Jesus until death, anyone who is not still studying and reflecting on Jesus's teachings is a "dropout." That is why so many are not experiencing the fullness of life or having more effect on the world. They have stopped being disciples. They are "Christian dropouts."

The remedy is a very simple. All anyone has to do is make a simple, easy, concrete choice. Just start studying.

Get acquainted with the Bible: For starters, we just need to pick up the Bible and begin reading. We can begin anywhere. I would suggest beginning with the Gospels and going on from there.

"What if I don't understand what I read?"

Well, if you don't understand, you will have questions. That is good, because then you can look for answers. When you get the answers, you will have learned something. That is forward motion.

"Yes, but where will I get the answers?"

It's not that hard. Try Googling. Get a Bible with lots of footnotes—like the *New American Study Bible,* the *Jerusalem Bible,* the *Oxford New Revised Standard Ecumenical Study Bible,* the *Ignatius Catholic Study Bible,* or the *Christian Community Bible, Pastoral Edition.*

You can also call someone: your pastor or someone who is in a group that reads and discusses the Bible. You can join such a group yourself. Or form one. Pope Francis wrote, "The study of the sacred Scriptures must be a door opened to every believer. Evangelization demands familiarity with God's word, which calls parishes to provide for a serious, ongoing study of the Bible, encouraging prayerful reading, both individual and communal" (*Joy of the Gospel*, 175).

We don't need to be experts. The Bible was written for ordinary people to read and understand. People like us.

Why don't we understand the Bible? The problem is very simple: Many of us don't understand the Bible because we have never read it. And when it is read to us at Mass, it frequently leaves us confused.

That is because all we hear at Mass are a few short passages selected from various books of the Bible and read out of context. That doesn't work unless we have some familiarity already with the whole book.

Could you turn on the television, watch a single, three-minute movie scene, then walk out and say you "understood" the movie?

The solution is just as simple. Read the Bible. Read each book of the Bible as a whole book, not as a collection of disconnected sayings. Read the whole Bible as a series of books that keep referring to each other, that cannot be understood completely except in relationship to each other. Once you are familiar with the whole, you will be able to understand the parts.

"But that means investing time, doesn't it?"

Yes, but who gave us time? And for what? Yes, we need to do some reading—like we did when we took courses in school. Students take homework for granted. If we prepare for Mass by looking at the Scripture readings ahead of time, then when we hear them read, we can just sit back and absorb them. Why not make Mass enjoyable?

What we are really talking about here is making the choice to be a real "disciple," a "student" of Jesus Christ. That is a simple choice, very concrete. And it is not that difficult. What does it cost to pick up the Bible and start reading it? And what do we believe—ah, here is the question—what do we believe we might get out of it?

The Scriptures are the *word of God*. Does that answer the question?

In *Rejoice and Be Glad* (156), Francis quotes the bishops of India: "Devotion to the word of God is not simply one of many devotions, beautiful but somewhat optional. *It goes to the very heart and identity of Christian life. The word has the power to transform lives.*"

Does that sound like a good reason to invest time?

How to pray using Scripture: Why do people say they "can't pray" over Scripture? Why do some say they don't know how to pray, period?

If "praying" is a problem let's not talk about praying. Let's talk about things we know we can do, like reading and thinking, and choosing. The best definition of "praying over Scripture" is *to read a passage from the Bible and think about it until you come to a decision about something you are actually able to do.*

Can you read? Can you think about what you have read?

"Yes, but it doesn't get me anywhere. I go blank."

Okay, "to think" is too abstract anyway. Can you ask some questions about what you read; like, "What does this mean? Who is Jesus talking to? What does he say to do? Why? What does this tell me about the way Jesus thinks? About the kind of person he is?"

Can you try to answer the questions?

"Yes, I can do that. But I don't get any of those great insights you're supposed to get. My answers don't seem to be worth much."

Fine, here's the key: if your answers don't seem to be worth much, forget about getting deep insights. Just get practical. Ask yourself, "*What can I do* to respond to what I've just read? What can I do that will *express in action* that I take seriously what I've read? That I believe it? When can I do this? How?"

These are all one practical question. When you answer it, you will have prayed over Scripture and prayed very successfully. At least, you will if you stay there until you make a *decision* and then actually do what you have decided.

These are the "three R's" of Scriptural prayer: *Read, Reflect, Respond.*

The words of God are not meant just to enlighten us; they are meant to cast light on a path. Jesus called himself, not just the Truth, but the "Way, the Truth and the Life" (John 14:16). His *truth* shows us the *way* that leads to *life.* His school is not a school of academic learning; it is a vocational school, a school for hands-on learning. The Bible is a handbook for action. If we do not read God's words as invitations to response, we will never understand them. If we do not read them with a view to making choices in response, we will be asking for directions without intending to go anywhere. When we do that, we lose contact with Jesus. Jesus speaks to those who want to follow.

"A highway will be there, called the holy way . . . It is for those with a journey to make . . ." (Isaiah 35:8, *Jerusalem Bible*)

St. Teresa of Avila, after explaining to her contemplative nuns seven levels of intimacy with God, ranging from bare acquaintance to the "spiritual marriage" and describing various levels of prayer, says at the end of *The Interior Castle,* "This is the reason for prayer, my daughters, and the purpose of this spiritual marriage: the birth always of good works, good works."

Teresa says, "The important thing is not to think much, but to love much." In prayer we should do whatever best stirs us to love. And love, she repeats over and over, "does not consist in feeling great delight but in desiring with strong determination to please God in everything. . . ." Love is shown in action.

So to pray well over Scripture, it doesn't matter what we feel, whether we get "turned on" or not, or even what great thoughts we get. What does matter is whether or not we find something we can act on, something to which we can respond in choices and in action. If we find that, we have prayed well.

This is the prayer of discipleship. It is down-to-earth and practical. Its focus is on learning new attitudes and values from Jesus Christ, understanding his reasons for them, and responding to him in practical, concrete decisions.

Not "Should I?" but "Could I?" Something very important: any decision we make must be something we are actually able to do. It is perfectly acceptable, even desirable, to let our hearts stretch out in desires without limit, longing for that total perfection and union that are still beyond our reach. It is good to beg God to change us. But to make sure our feet are on the ground and actually moving over it, we need to end our prayer with a decision to do something it is actually in our power to do right here and now.

Don't just ask, "What should I do?" Ask, "What could I do?"

When we can't do what we should, then we should do what we can. We take a small step that will help us get closer to our goal. All Jesus asks is forward motion. For example, if we can't immediately break a habit of using bad language, we can fine ourselves every time we do. At fifty cents—or five dollars—a word, we will clean up our vocabulary fast!

It is better to promise a pebble and deliver than to pledge the moon and just dream about it. When Jesus urges us to "sell everything" in order to buy the "treasure hidden in a field," he doesn't exclude the installment plan. Pope Francis says, "Grace, precisely because it builds on nature, does not make us superhuman all at once. Ordinarily, once we are attracted and empowered by his gift, it takes hold of us and transforms us progressively" (*Rejoice and Be* Glad, no. 50).

To pray over Scripture, then, all we have to do is *read a passage from the Bible* and *think about it* until we *come to a decision* about something we are actually able to do.

The key words are "until" and "able."

And especially, "do!"

Making the Choice to Be a Disciple

Anyone can be a disciple of Jesus Christ. Everyone is invited. We just have to choose it.

The choice really comes down to just one thing: the choice to give it some time. If we choose to invest time in learning from Jesus Christ, we are choosing to be disciples. If we don't choose to invest any time, we are choosing not to be disciples. It is as simple as that. Pope Francis says, "For each disciple, it is essential to spend time with the Master, to listen to his words, and to learn from him always" (*Rejoice and Be Glad,* 150).

How much time we invest has something to do with
it. Someone who only invests the time it takes to listen to
the Scripture readings at Mass is hardly serious enough to
be called a "student" of Jesus Christ. But we don't have to
spend five hours a day reading theology either. What does
it take to be authentically a disciple of Jesus?

The reality of discipleship is not measured by hours
but by seriousness. Learning from Jesus is less a matter
of extended periods than of constant preoccupation. A
disciple of Jesus Christ is always, in one way or another,
reflecting on his words, making the responses they call for,
cultivating the attitudes Jesus teaches, living out the values
he exemplifies, striving for the goals he proposes.

We are not fully, authentically disciples of Jesus until
our life is *characterized* by reflection on his words and
example. A disciple is someone who is always learning and
always applying what has been learned in order to learn
some more. A disciple automatically, spontaneously, even
unconsciously thinks with the thoughts and images of
Jesus, speaks with the vocabulary of Jesus, sees everything
through the eyes of Jesus, judges everything by the light of
his teachings, compares everything to his example.

The disciples of Jesus are so filled with the words and
images of Scripture that in everything they do and say, their
Christianity is as evident as their nationality. They speak with
a Christian accent. Their friends catch on after a while to
the fact that, no matter what situation arises, they are going
to react to it from a background of scriptural principles
drawn from the example and words of Jesus. And they do
this, more often than not, without explicitly mentioning
Jesus at all. They reflect him more than they refer to him.

For discipleship to permeate and characterize our life
in this way, formal fixed periods of study are necessary, of
course—not necessarily academic study, but time given
to reading, to listening to tapes or speakers, to reflection,

to meditation and prayer, to liturgy, to self-evaluation, to "progress reports" and coaching through the sacrament of Reconciliation or in spiritual direction. Some people have more time to give to this than others. And at some periods in our lives we need to give more time than at others. But one thing is certain: to be disciples we have to give enough time to be able to say with credibility that we are seriously studying the words and example of Jesus Christ, that we are real students of his. If we don't have time to give to this, we need to take a long, hard look at our priorities.

Checking the Foundation

If we can't find time to be disciples, we need to go back and look again at the "act of life-giving despair" that was the foundation of our decision to be Christian. Is Jesus an "extra" in our life? Can we get along without him? Can we get along without really knowing what he teaches—in depth and in breadth?

The key to everything is time. If we don't spend time learning from Jesus, how can he, as Light of the World, save us from the infecting darkness of the culture in our family and social life, business and politics? Is it going to be by magic?

In the Ten Commandments God prescribed a weekly day of leisure: the Sabbath. This Commandment was a pedagogical device. According to the rabbis, the purpose of the Sabbath is to teach us that human beings are different from the rest of creation. Everything else in the universe gets its reason for existence, its *raison d'être,* from what it contributes to the functioning of the planet. For that reason, nothing in nature "rests" unless there is a reason for resting or no present need to work. The sun comes up every day, the grass grows, and animals hunt for food until they are tired or satisfied.

But humans are told to rest one day a week, whether there is work to be done or not, whether they are tired or not, whether there is any reason for resting or not, and whether they like it or not. The purpose of the day of leisure is to make us realize that we humans do not find our reason for existing in our work. Work is an important element of human life but not life's ultimate purpose. As persons we are designed for direct, immediate relationship with God. We are made for God. We exist for God. Our lives have absolute value from that fact alone, whether we seem to contribute anything to the wellbeing of the planet or not.

To get that point across, God told us that on one day a week we should do no work—that is, do nothing just because it has to get done (barring emergencies, of course). That is what work is: something we do that is not just for fun. Through the Sabbath observance, we express and experience the truth that human beings do not exist just to get things done but to live in relationship with God.

When we are so absorbed by our work and duties that we have no time for discipleship, no time to cultivate relationship with God through deepening knowledge and love, and no time to sit at the feet of Jesus as Teacher, then we lose what the Sabbath law was established to give, regardless of what we do or don't do on Sundays. When we have no leisure time to spend on God (and a quick trip to Sunday Mass is not leisure time), we are missing the lesson of the Sabbath observance, and we are not keeping the Commandment, "Remember to keep holy the Sabbath day." We are not learning to be what we are.

The law of leisure is a very serious Commandment. Not to keep it is very serious. The law of Sabbath leisure was made for a purpose, and when we do not keep the law, then whether we are guilty of sin or not, its purpose is not achieved in our lives. And we are the poorer for it.

Some people are not free to keep the Sabbath. Slaves, for example. And many people today feel they are slaves of an economic system that requires them to work without respite. Many businesses stay open on Sunday. Many people work two jobs. Many who have only one job have other responsibilities that seem to take up every minute of their time, every day of the week. Those who are caught in these situations must judge for themselves whether they are truly slaves or free. If they are not free, they are not guilty of breaking the law of the Sabbath. But guilty or not, they will still suffer the loss of what the Sabbath was designed to give. And that is a serious loss.

When, however, we are free to take the leisure called for by the Sabbath observance, but our own priorities prevent us from keeping this Commandment, we have to ask ourselves whether something has come loose in our guidance system. We might be living for the wrong goals in life. We might be spending all our energy propelling ourselves to nowhere.

For practical purposes "time" and "life" on this earth are the same thing. Time begins for each of us when our life begins. And when our life ends, that is the end of our time. This means God gives us time for whatever purpose he gives us life. Therefore, if we say we "don't have time" to spend on learning to know and love God, we are saying we don't have life for that purpose. Then what do we have life for?

The truth is, God gave us both life and time for one precise purpose: that we might cultivate relationship with himself. Since that is all we have life for, we could argue it is all we really have time for.

Pope Francis says we have to "realize the need to stop this rat race and to recover the personal space needed to carry on a heartfelt dialogue with God. Finding that space may prove painful, but it is always fruitful. Sooner or later,

we have to face our true selves and let the Lord enter"
(*Rejoice and Be Glad,* 29).

Without giving time to discipleship, we won't know
enough about God to love him as we should or serve him
as he desires. If we want to live a Christian life, then, the
second step is to choose to *lead a life characterized by reflection
on the message of Jesus.*

That is the choice to be a *disciple.*

QUESTIONS FOR REFLECTION AND DISCUSSION

1. 1. Can I say I am living a life "characterized by
   reflection on the message of Jesus"? Would I call
   myself his disciple?
2. What concrete actions could I take that would make
   me a real "student" of Jesus? When, where, and how
   could I begin?
3. If God asked me what really keeps me from reading
   Scripture every day, how would I answer? (He is
   asking right now, by this question).

STEP 3

THE CHOICE TO BE A PROPHET

The third step into that "life to the full" Jesus came to give is the choice *to make everything in my life and lifestyle bear witness to Jesus Christ.*

That is what it means to accept my baptismal commitment as a *prophet.*

To do this I have to die to fear of standing alone by making personal decisions.

A Christian prophet is not someone who foretells the future but someone who creates it.

Prophets lead the Church into the future by embodying the future in their own lives. The actions of the prophets are embodied previews of a new level of morality, a new expression of grace, a new response to the needs of our times that may become the official stance of the Church after the witness of the prophets is received.

The problem with being a prophet is that no one likes to stand alone: not even—and especially not—before the silent tribunal of one's own heart. We don't like to take the responsibility of making deep moral decisions all by ourselves. We prefer to delegate decisions of conscience to a committee.

The easiest, most common way to do this is just to follow the crowd. That is called "cultural conformity."

A second, deceptively religious way is to abdicate personal judgment in favor of law-observance. That is called "legalism." The technical name for it is "Phariseeism." Phariseeism is religion focused on laws.

If we want to be prophets, we have to break free of cultural conformity and go beyond law-observance. In both cases we are giving up the sense of security that is found in the middle of a crowd. We are accepting the challenge to stand alone. We were consecrated in Baptism to do this.

As Pope Francis describes it,

> Like the prophet Jonah, we are constantly tempted to flee to a safe haven. It can have many names: individualism, spiritualism, living in a little world, addiction, intransigence, the rejection of new ideas and approaches, dogmatism, nostalgia, pessimism, hiding behind rules and regulations. We can resist leaving behind a familiar and easy way of doing things. Yet the challenges involved can . . . serve to bring us back to the God of tenderness, who invites us to set out ever anew on our journey. (*Rejoice and Be* Glad, 134)

What Is a Prophet?

In general, a prophet is anyone who "professes" the truth of God publicly. We exercise our baptismal consecration as prophets every time we make the sign of the cross in public, enter a church, or genuflect to the tabernacle. We are living up to our commitment as prophets when we speak up in defense of the truth or live out the teachings of Jesus in action. Whatever is an act of Christian witness is an act of prophesy, of professing faith in Jesus Christ. To be a witness and to be a prophet are one and the same thing. Pope Francis says,

> We are all called to be holy by living our lives with love and by bearing witness in everything we do, wherever we find ourselves. . . The holiness to which the Lord calls you will grow through small gestures. (*Rejoice and Be* Glad, 14, 16)

We can also say a Christian prophet is someone who *takes the general, abstract principles of the Gospel and applies them creatively to the concrete circumstances of a given time and place.*

Jesus seldom, if ever, made rules. He taught principles instead.

A *principle* is defined (by Aristotle) as "that from which something begins." A moral principle is a statement from which moral reflection begins. For example, when Jesus says, "Love one another as I have loved you," that is a principle. We can't just go out and do it; we have to think about what it means in practice and make some judgments. Whom am I called to love? What does it mean to love this particular person, here and now, as Jesus has loved me?

Principles require us to think—to decide for ourselves—what these words call us to do in the concrete, practical reality of our own lives. Principles get us started, but before we can act, we have to come to some concrete decision.

We think of laws, on the other hand, as statements that end moral reflection. Laws tell us exactly what to do. We assume no further reflection is needed, that we should just do what the law says. In a general way we can say that moral reflection begins with principles and ends (for a community, at least) with laws.

This may be standard practice, but it is not really the Christian way of observing laws. Nothing ever exempts a Christian from thinking. We are required to make personal judgments in every individual case, applying the law to the reality we are dealing with and asking whether in this particular situation doing what the law says will bring about the result the lawgiver intended and desires. If not, the common teaching in the Church is, "It is bad to obey the law!" So the prophets don't.

Cardinal Amleto Giovanni Cicognani, later Secretary of State under Popes John XXIII and Paul VI, said it clearly:

> Because human actions which are the subject of laws are individual and innumerable, it is not possible to establish any law that may not sometimes work out unjustly. Legislators, however, in passing laws, attend to what commonly happens, although to apply the common rule will sometimes work injustice and defeat the intention of the law itself. *In such cases it is bad to follow the law; it is good to set aside its letter and follow the dictates of justice and the common good.* (*Canon Law,* Newman Press, 1934, pages 12–21 and 608–628. This is the teaching of St. Thomas Aquinas, Summa Theologica, Part II–II, Question 120, article 1.)

The prophets understand it is clearly disobedience to follow the letter of the law in a way that is contrary to the mind and purpose of the lawgiver. But frequently lawgivers who are remote from the situation do not see that following their law in a particular case will frustrate its purpose. That is when they stone the prophets. They call the prophets disobedient for being more obedient than the "legalists" or those who are less attentive and less perceptive than they are.

There are other situations that call for a law where none exists. Then the witness of the prophets frequently becomes a preview of law. In the Church, for example, when the general principle, "Love one another as I have loved you," was not specific enough to tell Catholics that racial segregation should be outlawed, the prophets stood up and took a stand on the Gospel. They stood on principle in the absence of adequate laws. Because of their witness, the bishops finally recognized that segregation was a failure to apply the teaching of Jesus to the concrete reality of the situation. So the bishops abolished segregation in Catholic schools and churches— and converted prophecy into law.

This had already happened in civil law. Between the principles of the Constitution and the law stood the prophets. If they had not applied American principles to the reality of racial discrimination and expressed this in their action—including civil disobedience—those principles would not have taken flesh in action or in law. Sometimes, before principles can be embodied in laws, they have to be embodied in acts of witness. Francis says that is how prophets create the future:

God is eternal newness. He impels us constantly to set out anew, to pass beyond what is familiar, to the fringes and beyond. He takes us to where humanity is most wounded, where men and women, beneath the appearance of a shallow conformity, continue to seek an answer to the question of life's meaning. (*Rejoice and Be Glad,* 135)

The Unwritten Laws of Practice

The word *law* can refer to more than explicit rules and regulations. What we call "unwritten laws" are simply what people expect of people in a given culture.

The most dangerous laws are the unwritten ones that proclaim by their absence that something is permissible when it is not. There was an unwritten law—common Christian practice—that said slavery was permissible when it was not. There was an unwritten law—the silent Christian acceptance of segregation—that said racial discrimination was permissible when it was not. What the Church does not say can have as much influence on our lives as what she does.

The voice that will break this silence—the only voice that can break it—is the voice of the prophets. The official voices in the Church—the pastors, the bishops, the hierarchy—are normally the voices of stabilizing authority, not of groundbreaking prophecy. Church officials are commissioned and charged to be public voices, not private ones. They speak for what is already accepted, already authorized, or already seen clearly enough to be authorized and legislated in the community. It is unfair to expect the voice of public authority to be also the voice of private inspiration.

And yet, sometimes official voices are prophetic. When bishops and pastors speak, not just as official teachers of approved doctrine and law, but also as active preachers of the Gospel, they frequently speak as prophets. Then they receive from their own flock as well as from the world a "prophet's reward"—resistance, rejection, and even persecution. Sometimes those Christians who were the most vocal about the need for obedience and law observance in the Church turn their coats and fight violently against the very authority they idolized.

How to Become a Prophet

Theologically, no Christian has to become a prophet; we were all made prophets—consecrated and empowered to be prophets—when we were anointed with chrism at Baptism.

But what we are and what we actually do are frequently out of step with each other. We do not become fully what we say we are until our doing matches our being. We do not enter into the reality of our baptismal consecration as prophets until we consciously recognize and accept, on a personal level, our commitment to bear prophetic witness.

What does that mean in the concrete? When are we really—personally and practically—committed to being prophets? It is well and good to say, "I commit myself to receiving prophetic insights!" but that doesn't mean we will receive them. We might want to apply creatively the general, abstract teachings of Jesus to the concrete circumstances of our own time and place, but will we recognize how to apply them? Will we actually see what needs to be done?

As we get specific here and begin to spell out the prophetic commitment, we are taking for granted that readers have already made the first two steps into the fullness of Christian life; that is, that all are already committed to living on the divine level of God as *Christians* and studying the mind and heart of Christ as his *disciples.*

A prophet acts visibly as the body of Jesus, the Word of God made flesh. In the prophet the words of Jesus are made flesh in action. It follows that to be prophets we must be committed to making Jesus Christ a partner in everything we do. And to do this we must be disciples. We cannot hope to see how the words of Jesus apply to life in our time and place unless we are familiar with those words.

We cannot apply the Gospel to life unless we are studying the Gospel. But granted the first two commitments, the commitment to being a prophet requires two other choices that are both serious and radical.

Changing the question: The first choice is to change our whole standard of morality. The prophet makes a deliberate decision *never to ask again just whether something is right or wrong, but whether it bears witness to the values of Jesus Christ.*

Saint John Paul II wrote, "Following Christ is the essential and primordial foundation of Christian morality. Jesus's way of acting, his words, his deeds and his precepts constitute *the moral rule of Christian life.* Christ's example, no less than his words, is *normative for Christians*" (*The Splendor of Truth,* 20; World Day of Peace address, January 1, 1993). Taken seriously, these words will revolutionize our moral standards. Prophets take them seriously.

The commitment to be a prophet is not a commitment to find the right answers. It is a commitment to ask the right questions. The prophet doesn't ask, "Is it wrong to speak like this, dress like this, spend money like this, spend time on this?" The prophet asks, "Does it bear witness to the values taught by Jesus if I do?"

The law-observer asks, "Is it wrong not to invite this person to the party?" the prophet says the question should be, "Does it bear witness to Jesus Christ if I leave that person out of the party?"

The law-observer asks, "Is it wrong to go along with this policy where I work?" The prophet says, "You can't approach it that way. Ask instead if it bears witness to Jesus Christ if you go along with it."

But don't oversimplify. We do not always bear authentic witness to Jesus by doing the most idealistic thing—even though more commonly we fail to bear witness when we don't. Jesus said we are to be "wise as serpents and simple as doves" (Matthew 10:16). Simple does not mean simplistic. There are usually many factors to take into consideration when we make a concrete moral decision. The prophet weighs them all. It is not an easy task. It calls for discernment.

Law-observers just stay within bounds, keeping their eyes on the channel markers, the Ten Commandments. Prophets keep their eyes on the "fixed star" that is Jesus. They navigate.

Law-observers relate only to rules. Prophets are ruled by relationships with persons.

Pope Francis says, "It is not a matter of applying rules or repeating what was done in the past, since the same solutions are not valid in all circumstances, and what was useful in one context may not work in another. Discernment liberates us from rigidity, which has no place before the perennial 'today' of the risen Lord."

> Discernment is not only necessary when we need to make crucial decisions. We need it at all times to heed the promptings of his grace and hear his invitations to grow. Greatness of spirit is manifested in simple everyday realities, striving for all that is great, better and more beautiful, while at the same time being concerned for the little things, for each day's responsibilities. (See *Rejoice and Be Glad,* 169, 173)

He adds: "For this reason, I ask all Christians not to omit, in dialogue with the Lord, a sincere daily 'examination of conscience.'"

The prophet learns by trial and error how to discern the truth. Often we can't know for sure whether we are right or not. That is why the prophet has to die to fear, beginning with the fear of being wrong.

A commitment to continual conversion: Being a prophet
involves a second choice: the commitment to continual
conversion.

Conversion is too vague a word. Suppose we pledged
ourselves right now to "continual conversion of life."
Would we know what we are promising to do? A year
from now, if asked, "Are you more converted to Jesus than
you were last year?" how would we answer?

"I don't know." "Maybe." "I suppose so." "I hope so."

So let's use a word that means something. Suppose we
commit ourselves to "continual change." Suppose we stand
before Jesus and say, "Lord, I promise I will make continual
changes in my lifestyle. I don't know how many; I don't
know how often. But I will start making changes, and I will
keep doing it." A year from now, if asked what changes we
have made, we will know exactly how to answer. Either there
will be concrete changes we can point to, or there won't be.

The commitment to make constant changes declares
what we will do. The commitment to keep asking what
bears witness to the values of Jesus declares *how* we will
do it. We will keep changing by examining everything in
our life and lifestyle under the light of the teaching and
example of Jesus. These are the two commitments that
make us prophets. The commitment to keep changing
gets us moving; the commitment to bear witness gives
us direction. Together with discipleship, they guarantee
prophetic insights: discovering new and creative ways to
apply the Gospel to life.

To be prophets, then, we need to begin looking
systematically into every element and expression of our
lifestyle, asking about each one: "How does this—or how
could this—bear witness to the teaching of Jesus?" We need
to look at how we spend our time, how we spend our
money, what we eat and drink, how we speak to people at
home and at work, how we dress and drive, the books on

our shelves and bed table. We need to evaluate the goals
we pursue and the means we use to achieve them; the
principles we follow and the policies we establish in our
profession. We need to begin reshaping and reordering our
lives—every element of our lifestyle—according to the
pattern taught and modeled by Jesus in the Gospels.

Are we willing to make these two commitments? If
we don't yet feel sufficiently mature as Christians to be
prophets, Jesus offers three reasons that might tell us why
(Parable of the Sower, Matthew 13:1):

The Beaten Path: Jesus said the first reason why the seed
of his word does not grow in our hearts is that it falls
on the "beaten path" of social conformity. Anything
Jesus teaches that is in contradiction to what "everyone"
is doing doesn't penetrate, doesn't even register with
us, because we take for granted that what everyone is
doing—especially if they are churchgoing Christians—
must be what Jesus teaches. We interpret what Christ
says by what Christians do instead of measuring what
Christians do by what Christ says.

Jesus said, "By their fruits you will know them"
(Matthew 7:16). But if we begin with the assumption that
the most common fruit on the market must be good fruit,
we are judging by an unreliable standard. By uncritically
swallowing the fruit of mediocre Christianity, we lose our
taste for the root, for the radical call of the Gospel. We rule
out any radical summons of Christ that here and now is
falling on a majority of ears that cannot hear it.

To break through the blindness of social conformity,
we have to take a pickax to the "beaten path." We have
to despair of reaching fulfillment by following the course
society, even our so-called Christian society, lays down for
us. We have to decide instead to give the person of Jesus
Christ as Savior an active role in every area and action of

our lives. This is a radical break with the culture, and it is the real decision to live God's divine life as a *Christian*.

The Rocky Ground: The second reason why the seed does not grow is that it falls on rocky ground that has no depth. The roots never take hold. When we do not reflect on the words of Jesus long enough to come to decisions, to make choices, our response falls short.

Nothing is really a part of us until we have made it our own by choices. No truth is rooted in our soul until we live it out in decisions. To commit ourselves to the "3 R's" of *reading, reflecting* on, and *responding* to the words of Jesus is to become a *disciple*. That is what gives our soul depth for the seed of God to grow.

Seed Among Thorns: Jesus pointed out a third obstacle to the growth of his word in our hearts: in untended ground, weeds and brambles start choking out the plant as soon as it begins to sprout. To let the word of God grow to fruition in us, we need to weed the garden— to get rid of whatever is in conflict with the ideals and goals, the attitudes and values of Jesus—because these obstacles block our sight, especially if they are not obvious enough to attract our notice. Weeding means deliberately attacking those desires and fears that may be blinding us, including those we think are not blinding us. We never know how dirty our glasses are until we clean them.

To find out what is holding us back we can start with what we are holding onto. Pick any desire you satisfy on a regular basis, any taste you gratify automatically or almost always: desire for food, sleep, comfort, certain kinds of recreation—sport, TV, reading, surfing the Internet—desire for attention, compulsive talking. Try giving up one or more of these for a week, just to see what it teaches you about yourself. Give up the drink before dinner, dessert, second helpings, fast driving, unnecessary shopping, anything that might have more of a hold on you than you realize.

Francis quotes Jesus: "Keep awake. Let us not fall asleep" (Mark 13:35).

> Those who think they commit no grievous sins against God's law can fall into a state of dull lethargy. Since they see nothing serious to reproach themselves with, they fail to realize that their spiritual life has gradually turned lukewarm. They end up weakened and corrupted. This corruption is worse than the fall of a sinner, for it is a comfortable and self-satisfied form of blindness. (*Rejoice and Be Glad,* 164, 165)

The best way to keep awake is to commit ourselves to continual change. First we promise God changes; then we start making them. In the process we discover what in our life needs to be changed.

We just start making changes, guided by the desire to make every visible element of our lifestyle express the attitudes and values of Jesus. Then we begin to see more and more.

A car's headlights illumine the road for three hundred feet ahead. If we never move the car we will never see farther than three hundred feet. Life is the same: if we want to see more, we have to move. To keep receiving prophetic insights, we have to get ourselves in gear.

That means action. It means physical, concrete choices: getting practical, applying the Gospel to real life, making our lives fit the Gospel instead of adapting the Gospel to fit our lives. It means acting on the light we receive, letting the light of Christ's teaching shine through flesh and blood. That is religion that can be seen, heard, tasted, and felt. That is what it means to be a *prophet*.

If we read the Gospel and admire it but do not act on what we see, we will never see anything more. But if we keep making changes, we will discover what obstacles are obscuring our vision. To maintain forward motion, we will have to remove whatever is holding us back. Then we will begin to see more, and more, and more.

Once we are doing what we can as disciples to learn the truth of Jesus, the obstacle to prophetic insight will be in the heart, not in the head. Clarity of mind is obscured by attachments of the heart. But if we purify our hearts by making our behavior conform to what we see in the Gospel, we will "see and understand." Jesus promised, "Blessed are the pure of heart—those who are single-minded in their desire to live life to the full—for they will see God" (Matthew 5:8).

That is the key to prophetic witness.

Making the Choice to Be a Prophet

The way to do this is very simple: just do it. We stand before Jesus Christ and promise that we will begin making changes in our life. And we promise we will make them by asking not what is right or wrong, but how we can make every choice and element of our lifestyle bear witness to the truth Jesus teaches and to the values he proclaims.

We can be systematic about it. We can begin going through our room, our house, or our worksite, looking at what is there and asking how it bears witness to the message of Jesus, what it says about our response to his Good News. We can look at how we spend our money, our time; how we choose our friends, our books, our cars, our clothes, our food and drink. If we do this with freedom of spirit, making it more like a hobby than a task, it can be enjoyable, even intriguing. We may discover how things with no immediately evident religious value testify in fact to God's love for the world and for us who use and enjoy his creation. We will never be bored again!

We may also find ourselves invited—and responding with joy—to a generosity beyond our wildest imaginings. We may experience ourselves living "life to the full."

The secret is to do this not as an obligation that arouses guilt but as a voluntary project that aims at a richer, fuller response to Jesus Christ.

We don't have to be heroic. We don't have to do it all at once. We just have to begin. Deciding to do that is the act of accepting our baptismal consecration as *prophets*.

QUESTIONS FOR REFLECTION AND DISCUSSION

1. What in my life shows unambiguously that I believe in Jesus? If I stopped believing in him today, what concrete choices would I make right now that would significantly (and visibly) change my lifestyle?
2. What specific changes could make my life bear better witness to the values of Jesus? When, where, and how will I make them?
3. How often do I go against the letter of the law in order to achieve the purpose of the lawgiver? When I keep rules, do I always ask what their purpose is?

STEP 4

THE CHOICE TO BE A PRIEST

**The fourth step into the fullness of life
in union with Jesus Christ is the choice
*to mediate the life of God to others.***

**That is what it means to accept my
baptismal consecration as *priest*.**

**To do this I have to die to the fear of
revealing myself through self-expression.**

Many of us grew up thinking of "religion" as living a good life, being a good person, pleasing God by good behavior, and being rewarded for this in heaven.

"Ministry" was for those called to be priests, nuns, deacons, lay missionaries or professionals in church work. Or for those who could devote themselves to part-time activities in the parish as Eucharistic ministers, visitors to the sick, members of the pastoral council.

We may never have thought of ourselves as consecrated to full-time ministry simply by the fact of Baptism. More than likely, we never thought about the words solemnly spoken to us at Baptism when we were anointed with chrism on the top of our heads:

> God the Father of our Lord Jesus Christ has freed you from sin, given you a new birth by water and the Holy Spirit, and welcomed you into his holy people. *He now anoints you with the chrism of salvation. As Christ was anointed Priest, Prophet, and King, so live always* as a member of his body, sharing everlasting life.

This is the "job description" of a Christian. The truth is, we were anointed *priests* by God himself. We were anointed to *minister.*

Chrism is from the same Greek word as "Christ," which translates the Hebrew word *Messiah*, which means "Anointed." By Baptism we became members of Christ the "Anointed One." As members of Christ we share in his messianic anointing as Prophet, Priest, and King. By this anointing we are consecrated, committed, and empowered to carry on the mission of Jesus as *prophets, priests,* and *stewards* of his kingship. That mission is our "job description."

We have seen what it means to be a prophet. Now we look at what it means to be a priest as a sharer by Baptism in the priesthood of Jesus. To accept this priesthood is the fourth step into the fullness of life.

Dying to Self-Enclosedness, Rising to Community

Priesthood is only intelligible within the context and acceptance of community. Those who receive the priesthood given in the sacrament of Holy Orders are never ordained for their private, personal benefit. They are ordained to serve the community. Ordination to priesthood is ordination to service, to ministry, to washing feet, and to being available in love. That is true of all priesthood.

The priesthood of Jesus, which is the only priesthood that remains (see Paul's letter to the Hebrews), was this. Jesus "did not come to be served but to serve and to give his life as a ransom for many" (Matthew 20:28). That is what priesthood is: serving as priests and dying as victims, giving oneself for the life of the world. All who are baptized into Christ are baptized into the priesthood of Jesus: consecrated to ministry, to service, to dying to self in order to live totally for God and other people in love. To be baptized is to accept the community dimension of our religion. It is to give ourselves as bread to be broken and eaten for the life of the world.

Jesus says to all the baptized what he said to Peter: "Do you love me? . . . Feed my sheep!" This is his great pastoral commandment (John 21:17). Pope Francis teaches, "For each of us, our brothers and sisters are the prolongation of the incarnation of Jesus: 'As you did it to one of these, the least of my brethren, you did it to me.'" (Matthew 25:40, *Joy of the Gospel,* 179)

We have to give up any idea that religion is a private affair. Francis reminds us, "God has chosen to call us together as a people and not as isolated individuals. No one is saved by himself or herself, individually, or by his or her own efforts. God attracts us by taking into account the complex interweaving of personal relationships entailed in the life of a human community." (*Joy of the Gospel,* 113)

Religion has not been a private affair since the Lord said to Cain, "Where is your brother Abel?" and Cain made the mistake of answering, "I do not know. Am I my brother's keeper?"

For Jews and Christians, religion has not been a private affair since God first made a Covenant with the twelve tribes of Israel. In the New Covenant also, Jesus entrusted his message to a community. He poured out the Holy Spirit on an assembly, not on a single individual. The word *church*—in Greek, *ekklesia*—means "assembly."

So to be authentic Christians we have to accept our relationship to God as relationship from within a community. We have to die to the idea that we can ever stand before God just as private individuals without any relationship to the rest of the community or to the rest of the human race. "Growth in holiness is a journey in community, side by side with others" (*Rejoice and Be Glad,* 141). This is especially true of Christians, because we were consecrated as "priests" in Baptism specifically to minister to others.

Mediating the Life of God

To minister as priests is to *mediate the life of God to others through love.* That sounds exalted. But what does it mean on ground level?

When God the Son came to be our priest, he took flesh. Jesus is the "Word made flesh": the Truth, Love, and Life of God made visible, embodied in physical actions, to give life to the world. When in Baptism we accept to continue his priesthood, we accept to do exactly the same thing: to let his invisible divine life within us take flesh in visible, physical expression. We dedicate ourselves to being the embodied expression of God's divine Truth, Goodness, and Love, so that in and through us Jesus can continue to give life to the world.

As "priests in the Priest," we dedicate ourselves to *expressing* our faith, to *expressing* our hope, and to *expressing* our love in ways that give life to every individual we meet.

Pope Francis tells us, "There is a kind of preaching which falls to each of us as a daily responsibility. It has to do with bringing the Gospel to the people we meet, whether they be our neighbors or complete strangers."

> This is the informal preaching which takes place in the middle of a conversation . . . It means being constantly ready to bring the love of Jesus to others, and this can happen unexpectedly and in any place: on the street, in a city square, during work, on a journey. (*Joy of the Gospel,* 127)

In our culture, which "suffers so much from anonymity," Francis says, "we who are the Church must stop whenever necessary to take a close look at others—to contemplate and empathize."

> Ordained and non-ordained ministers can make present in our world the fragrance of Christ's closeness and his personal gaze. The Church should be intent on initiating everyone—priests and laity—into this "art of accompaniment" so that all of us will learn always to remove our sandals before the sacred ground of the other (see Exodus 3:5). We need to give to our journeying together a healthy sense of closeness, characterized by a respectful and compassionate way of looking at each other that heals, liberates, and encourages growth to maturity in the Christian life. (*Joy of the Gospel,* 169, my translation)

When we give expression in physical words to the invisible truth that is in our minds by faith, we are using our human bodies to mediate truth to others. When the invisible ideals in our hearts become a spoken word of witness in our actions, our bodies become the medium through which the divine goodness of God is communicated physically to others. The spiritual words God is speaking in our hearts take flesh when we speak them with our lips. To let our bodies become the medium through which God shares his truth and reveals his goodness to others is to mediate life in love. That is priesthood.

The same is true of all the ways in which we embody God's love to others: when we express our love sexually to our spouse, or express it in nonsexual ways physically to others; when we care for the sick, give help to the poor, show compassion to those who are afflicted, or simply smile at the people whom we serve at work—or who serve us—in all this we mediate the love of God to others by letting his love take flesh in our actions. That is priesthood.

Constant self-expression is the key to priesthood, provided we are aware that the self we are expressing is the self united to Jesus, the divine self that we became by becoming one with the Son of God in Baptism, members of his body and temples of his Spirit.

> We need a spirit of holiness capable of filling both our solitude and our service, our personal life and our evangelizing efforts, so that every moment can be an expression of self-sacrificing love in the Lord's eyes. In this way, every minute of our lives can be a step along the path to growth in holiness. (*Rejoice and Be Glad,* 31)

To be a priest is to dedicate our humanity to being the self-expression of God.

Fear of Self-Expression

Why don't we express what is inside of us? Say something to people when we see they are depressed? Break the ice and give a smile to someone we are dealing with mechanically? Why don't we compliment people every time we see something good in them?

Why are we so reluctant to talk about our religion, our prayer, our spiritual experiences, the feelings we have for God? Why are we afraid to pray aloud with others, even with our family and closest friends? Why do we hang back from praying intimately with our spouse? From telling our children what we feel—not just think—about Jesus? Why are we so embarrassed about praying with others in our own words, spontaneously?

Self-Expression in Liturgy

At Mass, why do we kneel at the back of the church as if we were not part of the ministering team? Or pick a spot as far from others as we can get? Why not pray shoulder-to-shoulder as a community?

There is a time to pray alone. For that Jesus tells us to go into our room, shut the door, and pray to our Father in private (Matthew 6:6). But if we try to make the Mass that kind of prayer, we neither participate authentically in Mass, nor are we authentically alone. We falsify both kinds of prayer.

Why don't we sing at Mass? Or join in the assembly's responses enthusiastically, as if we were celebrating instead of just enduring? Why don't we participate like priests who are a part of the action, taking responsibility as ministers for the impact the liturgy is having on others as well as on ourselves?

Is it because we are there, not to serve but to be served? Do we think the ordained priest is there to minister and we are just there to be ministered to? Do we realize that all the baptized are priests charged to celebrate Mass just as officially as the ordained are? Do we think the ordained priest can "make the Mass happen" without us? The ordained priest has his special role, but alone he cannot make the Mass be for the congregation what it should be and do for the congregation what it should do. For that the whole congregation has to participate "fully, actively and consciously" (words of the bishops at Vatican II) so that the Mass may *be and be experienced* by all as what it authentically is.

A dead congregation at Mass is the sign of a dying parish. St. Paul describes the Mass as a communal enterprise, something the whole community has a hand in creating:

> When you assemble, one has a psalm, another an instruction, a revelation, a tongue, or an interpretation ... Two or three prophets should speak, and the others discern. But if a revelation is given to another person sitting there, the first one should be silent. For you can all prophesy one by one, so that all may learn and all be encouraged.... (See 1 Corinthians 14:26–32)

This description of what the early Christians did at Mass might sound very foreign to us. But it is consistent with Paul's teaching about the anointing we received at Baptism. Everyone anointed in Baptism to serve as *prophet, priest,* and *steward* of Christ's kingship is given gifts of ministry through the outpouring of the Holy Spirit:

> To *each individual* the *manifestation of the Spirit is given for the common good:* the expression of wisdom, knowledge, faith, gifts of healing, miracles, prophecy, discernment of spirits... But one and the same Spirit produces all of these, distributing them individually to each person as he wishes. (See 1 Corinthians 12:7)

The ways we share our gifts at Mass change over the ages, but the call to active, creative participation in liturgy and in the life of the Church is foundational. It is the truth upon which liturgy is built. The Church Saint Paul teaches us to be is a Church in which there are many different kinds of ministries, but every single member is a minister. Everyone receives the outpouring of the Holy Spirit, and everyone shares the gifts of the Spirit with others in a common ministry of "building up the body of Christ" in love (Ephesians 4:12–16). There are apostles and prophets; teachers, healers, and helpers; administrators and leaders; speakers in tongues and interpreters of tongues (see 1Corinthians 12:27–31). And there are many other gifts and ministries Paul doesn't list. But everyone is gifted by the Spirit, and everyone is called to share that gift in ministry. That is the law of life for those who live by the Spirit: to *share in* is to *share with*. There is no purely private, personal, individualistic religion in the body of Christ. All receive life, give life, and grow in life through the self-expression of the whole body and every one of its members.

The Mass is the prayer of the Church, and the Church is a community of priests. Jesus has "made us to be a kingdom, priests serving his God and Father." We are all "living stones, built into a spiritual house, to be a holy priesthood, to offer spiritual sacrifices acceptable to God through Jesus Christ" (Revelation 1:6; 1Peter 2:4–9).

If we are conscious of our priesthood at Mass, we will be more conscious of it outside of Mass. Because Eucharist was identified at the Second Vatican Council as "the source and summit of the Christian life" ("The Church," no. 11), what we do at Mass—what we express and experience there—has a great deal to do with the way we will perceive and express ourselves as Christians at work and at home, in our social lives, and in all our

activities. If we consciously minister to others at Mass,
it will become natural for us to see everything we do as
priestly ministry and service. We will be aware that in
everything we do, we are called to "offer our bodies as
a living sacrifice," our "flesh for the life of the world"
(Romans 12:1; John 6:51). We do this together with
Jesus—*through him, with him,* and *in him*—as he offers
himself *with us, in us,* and *through us* for the life of the
world.

When we are fully conscious of being present at Mass
as ministers and of ministering during Mass as priests, then
outside of Mass we will continue to mediate divine life
to every person we deal with by surrendering to let Jesus
reveal his light, express his love, and give his life in and
through all our physical human words and actions.

It was for this that God gave us the Holy Spirit at
Baptism: "to equip the holy ones—all the baptized—for
the work of ministry, for building up the body of Christ .
. . to grow to maturity, to the measure of the full stature of
Christ . . . from whom the whole body, . . . as each part is
working properly, promotes the body's growth in building
itself up in love" (see Ephesians 4:11–16).

Dying to Fear—Rising to Ministry

A priest is someone who has accepted the ministry of
mediating the life of God to others. And every Christian
is consecrated to this priesthood by Baptism. So we
should make it our constant ministry to "build up the
body of Christ" in love.

Whatever excuses we offer for not expressing our
religious devotion to others, the root reason is fear: fear
of self-revelation, fear of becoming vulnerable through
self-expression, fear of nakedness. This is a fear we must
overcome.

This is not always fear of being seen as we are. It may be fear of being seen as we are not, fear that we will be perceived by others as freaky. We are afraid that if we express what is deep within us, the expression won't really match what we feel, won't do it justice, won't be understood, or simply won't be acceptable to the people we are with.

Or we may be afraid that something deep within us will be desecrated by nonappreciation. Jesus had something to say about not tossing pearls to people who can't appreciate them (Matthew 7:6).

Sometimes we are just afraid of being identified with the kind of people who "push religion" or whose religious emotionalism we find distasteful. We don't want to look like them.

Not to worry. If you have been "turned off" by inappropriate religious expression, there is no danger you will sin by excess in the revelation of yourself. Those who are keenly aware of the cliff don't go near the edge. Those who worry about falling into sentimentality or emotionalism in their religious expression never come close to it.

The Nakedness of God

If the reasons we give for not revealing ourselves to others are valid, then God should never have taken flesh in Jesus.

God knew that if he let his true self be seen—if he revealed himself to the human race as he really is—he would not be appreciated. His truth would be misunderstood. He would be misunderstood and rejected.

God also knew there was no way his human self-expression, even in Jesus, the Word made flesh, could begin to do justice to the divine truth and beauty of his Person. If we hold back from revealing our deepest, most intimate selves because we fear the desecration of nonappreciation, what must God have felt at the prospect of letting the inmost truth of his being—his goodness, his beauty as the Word, the second Person of the divine Trinity—appear in the limitations of human flesh before the eyes of the human race?

Is it too much to ask, as St. Paul does, that we should "let the same mind," the same attitude, be in us "that was in Christ Jesus: who, though he was in the form of God, emptied himself, being born in human likeness, found in human form?" (see Philippians 2:5–8)

If God was not afraid to take the risk of revealing himself in Jesus, the Word of God made flesh, should we be afraid of revealing ourselves by giving human expression to the words he speaks in our hearts?

The fourth step, then, is the commitment *to mediate the life of God to others* by *giving expression* through our human words and actions to the light and love of God that are within us.

To do this we have to die to our fear of self-expression, to any compulsion to keep our religion a private affair. We have to embrace the ministry of self-revelation, the ministry of the Word made flesh.

When we do this, we will be free to let our human flesh be what it was consecrated at Baptism to be: the body of Christ mediating the life of God to others, his flesh and ours given for the life of the world.

That is priesthood. It is dying to self in order to live totally for God and other people in love. It takes the form of self-expression.

We are called to it. If we are obedient to that call, it can lead us "to the point of death—even death on a cross."

To decide to do that is to accept our baptismal consecration as *priests*.

QUESTIONS FOR REFLECTION
AND DISCUSSION

1. Why am I so afraid to express my thoughts, my feelings about God? To pray out loud with others? Share what I think about a Scripture passage? Talk about my experience of God?
2. In what concrete ways can start giving physical expression to the divine truth and love that are within me? Concretely, how, when, where do I choose to do this? With whom?
3. Am I going to keep sitting where I always sit at Mass? Am I going to sing? Make the responses more enthusiastically? If not, why not?

STEP 5

THE CHOICE TO BE A STEWARD

The fifth step into the fullness of life in Christ is the choice to *take responsibility for transforming the world as a steward of the kingship of Christ.*

This is what it means to accept my baptismal consecration as *king.*

To do this I have to die to any sense of hopelessness or discouragement about the effect I can have on the world.

Jesus's first recorded preaching was, "The kingdom of God has come near." His last recorded act was to turn over to us the responsibility for establishing it (Matthew 4:17; 28:18).

Mark calls his Gospel "the good news of Jesus Christ" (1:1). Jesus began to describe the good news when he stood up in the synagogue of Nazareth to read. He chose the text:

"The Spirit of the Lord is upon me, because he has anointed me to bring good news to the poor . . . to proclaim liberty to captives and recovery of sight to the blind, to let the oppressed go free." . . . Then he said to them, "Today this Scripture passage is fulfilled in your hearing." (Luke 4:18)

It is still being fulfilled. The mission of Jesus as Messiah was to proclaim the kingdom of God as Prophet, to win it as Victim and Priest on the cross, and to reign over it as King for all eternity. But in the time frame of this earth, the kingdom Jesus won is still being extended throughout the world. The last thing Jesus did before ascending into heaven was turn over to us the mission of establishing his reign over all creation:

"All authority in heaven and on earth has been given to me. Go, therefore, and make disciples of all nations, baptizing them in the name of the Father, and of the Son, and of the Holy Spirit, and teaching them to obey everything I have commanded you. And remember, I am with you always, until the end of the age." (Matthew 28:18)

The fifth step into the fullness of life is to take responsibility for carrying out that command as stewards of his kingship.

The Best of Both Worlds

To "make disciples of all nations, teaching them to obey everything I have commanded you," does not mean simply teaching Christian doctrine all over the world. It means to establish God's reign over every area and activity of human life on earth by impregnating everything people do with the attitudes and values, the principles and priorities Jesus modeled and taught. This is God's "plan for the fullness of time: to gather up all things in him, things in heaven and things on earth" (Ephesians 1:10)—a plan Jesus will realize by working *with us, in us,* and *through us* as his risen body in the world.

We are charged to transform everything people do on this earth—in family and social life, in church, business, and politics—by bringing everything under the life-giving reign of Christ.

But it is not our mission to impose restrictive religious rules on activities natural to life in this world. We don't falsify the nature of business, politics, education, or family life by directing these to some artificial "religious" end instead of to their natural goal and purpose. Above all, we don't believe in putting the Church in charge of things the Church was never meant to be in charge of.

What we do intend is to bring the light and love of Christ into everything people do so that every activity people engage in might be more authentically, more fully, more fulfillingly, what it was intended to be in the first place—and more.

Grace means sharing in God's divine life through union with Jesus Christ. It makes us and everything we do divine. Grace lifts up every human activity to the level of God's own activity and fruitfulness. Grace never destroys—or diminishes—nature. What Jesus said about the law God gave to the Chosen People through Moses—"Do not think I have come to abolish the law or the prophets. I have come not to abolish but to fulfill" (Matthew 5:17)—he also says about every human action and enterprise transformed by grace. Christians acting in union with God by grace respect the true, natural purpose of what they are trying to transform. They leave nature intact. God the Redeemer does not act in contradiction to God the Creator.

When Jesus' mother told him at the wedding feast of
Cana, "They have no wine," he didn't answer, "Good; they
ought to be drinking lemonade!" No, he poured wine—
and in abundance (John 2:1).

The six jars Jesus had the servants "fill to the brim" each
held twenty gallons of water. Jesus turned it all into wine.
Think of the effect an additional 120 gallons of wine had
on that little country wedding feast! There could not have
been more than a hundred people present, and all had
drunk plenty already. Jesus didn't just turn water into wine;
he turned a wedding feast into an unforgettable experience.

When Jesus did this, John says he "revealed his glory,
and his disciples believed in him!"

What does that mean? As his disciples, they already
believed in him. It must mean that the disciples finally got
a hint of what Jesus really came to do on earth. He came
to have the same effect on the world that 120 gallons of
choice wine had on a little country wedding feast.

They are still talking about that wedding in Cana!

The wedding feast remained a wedding feast. But it
was transformed. In the same way, the "new wine" of Jesus
(Matthew 9:17) will transform gloriously every area and
activity of human life on earth.

Christian business will be characterized by excellence—
and by concern for the neighborhood, country, and planet.
Christian education will teach people to think—with minds
open to everything that is true and good and beautiful.
Christian politics will promote the common good—of all
people on earth. Christian recreation will truly "re-create"
strength and energy, not just anesthetize with mindlessness.
And in all things the unannounced but unobscured,
invisible but undeniable presence of Jesus, will inebriate
with something other than wine all who drink it in.

When the bishops at the Second Vatican Council
wanted to "explain to everyone" how they understood the

presence and activity of the Church in the world of today, they began with the sentence:

> The joys and hopes, the griefs and anxieties of the people of this age, especially those who are poor or in any way afflicted, these too are the joys and hopes, the griefs and anxieties of the followers of Christ. The truth is, nothing genuinely human fails to raise an echo in our hearts, for [the Church] is a community of human beings. (*Joy and Hope:* "The Church in the Modern World")

This sounds very much like the way Jesus introduced himself in Nazareth: "He has sent me to bring good news to the poor, to proclaim liberty to captives and recovery of sight to the blind, to let the oppressed go free" (Luke 4:16). God knows our needs, our "joys and hopes, griefs and anxieties." Pope Francis says God, who gave us our human hopes and desires, wants us to enjoy life on earth.

> It is no longer possible to claim that religion should be restricted to the private sphere and that it exists only to prepare souls for heaven. We know that God wants his children to be happy in this world too, even though they are called to fulfilment in eternity, for he has created all things "for our enjoyment" (1 Timothy 6:17); that is, the enjoyment of everyone. It follows that Christian conversion demands reviewing especially those areas and aspects of life "related to the social order and the pursuit of the common good." (*Joy of the Gospel,* 183)

God's plan for the "fullness of time," St. Paul tells us, is "to bring all things in the heavens and on earth into one under Christ's headship" (Ephesians 1:9, *New American*

Bible, 1970). Jesus came, not to polarize human life between "religious" activities and "secular," between values that are "eternal" and "temporal," between concern for what is of this world and what belongs to the next. Jesus came to unify things, to unify our outlook and our goals, to bring together everything we do under one, single, driving purpose in life: to make everything better in family and social life, business and politics, by bringing every area and activity of human life under the life-giving reign, not of "religion," but of God.

This is purity of heart, single-mindedness. Our religious focus is all encompassing while, paradoxically, respectful of boundaries. To be a "steward of the kingship of Christ" means to preserve nature as a prerequisite for transforming it by grace.

Francis says,

> An authentic faith always involves a deep desire to change the world, to leave this earth somehow better that we found it. We love this magnificent planet on which God has put us, and we love the human family which dwells here, with all its tragedies and struggles, its hopes and aspirations, its strengths and weaknesses. The earth is our common home and all of us are brothers and sisters.... The Church cannot and must not remain on the sidelines in the fight for justice. All Christians are called to show concern for the building of a better world. (*Joy of the Gospel,* 183)

In our day the Church is calling us to focus on "the ecological commitments which stem from our convictions." Pope Francis calls for an "ecological spirituality" that "can motivate us to a more passionate concern for the protection of our world . . . to care for nature and for the most vulnerable of our brothers and sisters." He calls this "an essential part of our faith," and insists that "our relationship with the environment can never be isolated from our relationship with others and with God."

> We must protect creation, for it is a gift which the Lord has given us. It is God's present to us. We are the guardians of creation. When we exploit creation, we destroy that sign of God's love. To destroy creation is to say to God: "I don't care." And this is not good: this is sin. (See "The Gift of Knowledge," General Audience, May 5, 2014; *Laudato Si'*—"On Care For Our Common Home," 64, 119, 216; John Paul II, World Day of Peace 1990, 15)

The Commitment to Stewardship

The question is, Do I want to be a part of this effort? Do I want to dedicate myself, my life, to establishing the reign of God on earth?

It is not a matter of changing jobs or of taking time away from what I do already in order to do something more. Christian stewardship is not limited to specialized vocations or identified with "religious activities." The most religiously effective person who ever lived, after Jesus, was Mary, who was "nothing but" a wife and mother. We establish God's reign by doing what we are already doing, but by doing it with a clear purpose in mind: to bring everything in heaven and on earth together into harmony under Christ's headship. It is not a matter of adding "religious activities," but of making every activity we engage in authentically religious.

The key word is responsibility.

A steward is more like a partner than a day-laborer. The steward's eyes are on the end to be accomplished, not on the end of the day.

The steward is "responsible," the one who "answers for" what is done and not done. That is what "response-ability" means.

When we were made one with Jesus as "King" at Baptism, we became responsible for bringing everything on earth under the reign of God. We are responsible for everything. We are not department heads or sub-managers. We report directly to Jesus himself. We are stewards of Christ the King, responsible for everything he wants done on earth.

For example, if we drive through substandard housing on our way to work, we see that as something we are responsible for changing. Substandard housing does not belong in the kingdom of God. If we see trash on the street, we are responsible for picking it up.

If someone threw trash in our backyard, we would pick it up, because we take responsibility for the way our yards look. The street is our Father's backyard.

However, being responsible for everything does not mean we have to do everything ourselves. That is manifestly impossible. If we tried to pick up all the trash on the streets where some of us live, we wouldn't have time for anything else! And we would neglect other, more important things for which we are responsible. We have to decide prudently how to use our time. We have to be selective. As managers, stewards, of the kingship of Christ, we accept responsibility for renewing everything on earth. But we make prudent judgments about how and where to invest our time and energies. And we pray for everything else.

We also involve ourselves in things other people are doing to establish the reign of God on earth, whether they consciously call it that or not. Everyone's effort is our effort; everyone's good cause is our cause, so long as it is moving in the direction of the fulfillment desired by God. As stewards of Christ's kingship, we accept and proclaim solidarity with all the legitimate strivings of the human race. We support them as much as we can. Jesus said, "Whoever is not against you is for you" (Luke 9:50).

To accept involvement with all who, explicitly or not, are working to establish the reign of God throughout the world is stewardship.

A Necessary Condition: Dying to Despair

The greatest obstacle to involving ourselves in efforts to transform the world is a combined sense of helplessness and hopelessness.

"There's nothing I can do about it." "Who's going to listen to me?"

"It's useless. Nothing can be done."

Frustration is hard to deal with. So we anesthetize ourselves with indifference. We pass from, "There's nothing I can do about it," to "I'm not going to get involved," to "It doesn't concern me."

We cop out, psychologically as well as physically. We just refuse to think about what is happening, or about how things ought to be, in contrast to how they are. We withdraw into isolationism. We mind our own business. We look after ourselves.

This doesn't have to take the form of a conscious refusal to take responsibility. It can be simply a matter of closing our eyes to the problems around us. In spite of his wife's complaints, a husband refuses to see any problem in their marriage. A mother closes her eyes to signs of sexual abuse in her children. An employee chooses not to take a hard look at dishonest policies and practices at the worksite. A priest won't listen to what is wrong with his ministry in the parish.

Whatever form it takes, we are refusing to take responsibility for the reign of God. And the root of our problem, if it is not just selfishness, is our failure to believe in the presence and power of Jesus.

The Apparent Absence of God

Part of the common Christian experience is a keen awareness of the absence of God.

It is not that God is really absent. It is just that we do not see him, may not feel his presence, and cannot understand why he isn't doing more than he seems to be doing to overcome evil in the world.

The Gospels emphasize the theme of Christ's leaving. When the people wanted to make him their king after he had multiplied bread in the wilderness, Jesus "withdrew to the mountain by himself." In a preview of his ascension into heaven, he left his disciples alone in their boat (symbol of the Church), rowing against the wind and the waves on a contrary sea (see Matthew 14:22–33; John 6:1–22).

This is typical of the experience of Christian life on earth. The Church is "battered by the waves"—especially those members who are trying to establish the reign of God in the frequently hostile environments of business, social life, and politics. Jesus does not appear to be in the boat. The "wind is against them," and they are "far from land."

Then he comes, walking across the sea, and they are terrified. They are not sure it is he. They think he is a ghost. They aren't really certain until, like Peter, they risk their lives by jumping into the stormy waves, trusting they can walk on the water!

That is what stewardship means: working to establish the reign of God in a world where the winds and currents of culture are frequently against the values Christ teaches—

working while "hoping against hope" (Romans 4:18), often without any perceptible help from Jesus.

And when Jesus does come—in the form of an idea, an inspiration—our first reaction is terror. "The risk is too great. There isn't the ghost of a chance. Does God think we can walk on water?" But we never know whether God is calling us until we answer. Jesus only calls those to walk on water who are willing to risk their lives by trying.

The steward is someone left in charge while the master is "away on a journey" (Matthew 25:14). While the master is away, the steward is charged to be faithful in taking responsibility for his kingdom, intent on the master's business until he comes again.

By definition, this means the steward feels abandoned and alone. The master is not there. The steward has to take full responsibility, make decisions, take decisive action, initiate changes and reforms, and persevere in doing this until the master returns.

"Take Courage! I Have Overcome the World!"

For perseverance, we need hope, a hope based on faith. The steward has to believe, not only that the master will return, but that he will return in triumph, that he has "overcome the world" (John 16:33).

To be faithful stewards of the reign of Christ, we have to believe that the war is already won, and we are just fighting the battles. We may win or lose this particular engagement, but fighting it is our contribution to the overall victory of God.

We are like players in a basketball game who are losing 104 to 0. The coach calls us over and says, "Get out there and play your hearts out. We can win this game!"

We look up at the time clock. Someone has covered it with a cloth.

If we go out there and play our hearts out, we have faith. It is faith to persevere in believing Jesus will triumph. It is fidelity to persevere in working to bring it about. Faithfulness is showing faith in action.

Belief in the master's return is our sustaining hope as we labor to implant his reign. We know the truth: Jesus has overcome the world. He will "come again in glory to judge the living and the dead, and his kingdom will have no end." (Profession of Faith at Mass; John 14:3)

But we know Jesus is not really absent. We know he is still present among us, living in our hearts, working in his Church, working in the heart of every human being who will listen even slightly to his voice. We know he is present, but we do not see him. We have to believe. We know he is working *with us, in us,* and *through us,* but we do not see the results. We have to trust. We know he has triumphed over sin and evil, but everything we see around us contradicts that. We have to persevere in faith and hope and in the love that keeps us working and spending our lives for him until he comes again.

That is what it means to be a "faithful steward" of the kingship of Christ: it means persevering in faith and fidelity until the King returns.

The Clearest Vision Is Blind Hope

To live as stewards of the kingship of Christ we have to die to hopelessness. We refuse absolutely to judge by appearances. We refuse to believe that nothing is getting better, that nothing can get better. We die to reliance on human efforts and rise up launched into greater human efforts than before by reliance on the power of God.

We do not look at what is happening around us to see whether Jesus is winning. As Christians we already believe absolutely that Jesus has overcome the world. We just look around us to see how we can make his victory visible in our time and place by getting involved.

We begin by trying to change our own environments— for example, to fill our family life with the "fruit of the Spirit": *love, joy, peace, patient endurance, kindness, generosity, faithfulness, gentleness,* and the *self control* of total surrender to God (Galatians 5:22).

We try to fill our social life with the values of Christ— to make everything we do for entertainment rebuild us and give us true joy of heart and to interact with our friends in a way that brings us closer to them in mind, heart, and soul.

In our professional environment—our job, school, or business—we work to establish a tone of peace, respect, and service to others. We urge policies that transform work into love. We strive to make working an experience of giving. We keep our hearts alive by feeding them all day long with the life-giving fire of generosity and helpfulness.

In our parish and diocese we notice what is missing or what could be done better. We speak out. We talk to the pastor and to the bishop. We join with others to bring about change.

In everything we are part of, we are willing to take a second look at goals and objectives, at ends and means, and to invite others to reexamine them. We ask how policies can be improved in the light of deeper and more universal human needs. We broaden our perspective, asking what more we can do to enhance our lives and the lives of others through what we already do, through what we are trained and committed to do.

We take ownership of our city, our neighborhood, our country. We look at how other people and groups are transforming society, sometimes with the best of intentions, sometimes with the worst. We listen for authentic voices of truth: not voices that try to impose their religious (or secular) faith on others, but voices that urge truth in the name of truth, love in the name of love, and peace in the name of peace—voices that speak to this world in the language of this world, proposing a way for the world that is based on truth and leads to life. And we join our voices to theirs.

We recognize such voices by their underlying conformity with the Way in which we hope, the Truth in which we believe, the Life that leads us into love.

Where no such voices are raised, we lift up our own, even when we seem to be voices crying in the wilderness. We rise up from the pit of hopelessness to assume responsibility for establishing the life-giving reign of Christ over every area and activity of human existence. We pledge ourselves to persevere as faithful stewards, in faith and fidelity, to embody faith in action, to work until Jesus comes again.

Begin by Noticing

To begin with, we commit to doing something easy. We simply train ourselves to start *noticing,* wherever we are, anything that needs to be changed, anything that is not completely right.

Normally, what people notice are the things for which they feel responsible. If we deliberately make a point of noticing everything around us that calls for change— whether we are able to do anything about it or not—that is an initial act of taking responsibility for everything we see; that is, for everything Jesus came to redeem. That is an experience of stewardship.

We notice everything, large and small. Pope Francis says, "Let us not forget that Jesus asked his disciples to pay attention to details."

> The little detail that wine was running out at a party ...The little detail that one sheep was missing ...The little detail of having spare oil for the lamps . . . The little detail of asking the disciples how many loaves of bread they had . . . The little detail of having a fire burning and a fish cooking as he waited for the disciples at daybreak.... (*Rejoice and Be Glad,* 144)

To notice is to take responsibility. When we start noticing everything, we realize we have accepted responsibility for everything. This responsibility is ours because at Baptism we were consecrated stewards of Christ's kingship, and he is "king over all the earth" (Psalm 47:2).

When responsibility leads us to notice and noticing lets us see what needs to be done, we are called to exercise *leadership.* Leadership is stewardship in action.

Only a few people have the authority that empowers them to get things done by others. But leadership does not require authority, any more than authority requires special gifts of leadership. People obey authorities out of commitment, but they follow leaders voluntarily because they believe the leader knows the way to go. Anyone who happens to see what needs to be done in a particular situation is, by that very fact, called to exercise leadership— and is consecrated to do so by Baptism as a *steward* of the kingship of Christ.

Taking responsibility for encouraging changes that transform society is the fifth and final step along what Pope Francis calls "the path of holiness." Taken together with the other steps, it brings us into the fullness of life.

QUESTIONS FOR REFLECTION AND DISCUSSION

1. In what concrete ways am I living up to my responsibility as a steward of Christ's kingship?
2. What do I notice that is inconsistent with God's reign in business, politics, family, or social life? In the media? What changes should authentic religion support in these areas?
3. In what specific, concrete ways could I work for change as a steward of the kingship of Christ? How, when, and where will I do this?

RESPONSE

Five Words—One Word

The only way to get anywhere is to start from where we are.

Each of these five steps is a choice, a word of response to our human cry for fulfillment, to the need of the human race, to God's invitation.

Each step depends on the one before it. To be *prophets,* we must be *disciples,* studying Christ's words as *Christians* who have accepted Jesus as Savior. To establish Christ's reign as *kings, stewards* of his kingship, we need his gentleness as victims and *priests.*

Suppose, for example, someone began with the fifth commitment—to transform society as a steward of Christ's kingship—without having committed to the other four steps. What would happen?

Those who work for peace and justice know that peace must take priority in their own hearts, or they will end up acting out of anger, polarizing people, resorting to violence, and accomplishing nothing. The axiom, "There is no peace without justice" cuts both ways: there can be no lasting justice unless it brings about lasting peace.

The lesson of Jesus is that love conquers the world. If we conquer by any other power, we have been defeated. This means we cannot take on the commitment to transform the world as stewards of Christ's kingship until we have surrendered ourselves to die for the world in love as victims of Christ's priesthood.

How do we get to this surrender? Five words give the answer.

1. Evangelization

We begin by accepting the Good News of Jesus as the Savior he really is—the one who does not just save us from sin but saves our whole life, every part of it, from veering off into destructiveness, distortion, mediocrity, and meaninglessness. This is the act of "life-giving despair" that grounds us in the deep realization that we will never do anything that is worthy of what we are unless we do it in partnership with Jesus acting *with us, in us,* and *through us.* When we truly believe in him as Savior and the only possible savior of our lives in this world, we will begin to depend on his saving guidance and power and so interact with him in everything we do. Then we will be consciously living the divine Life of God. Then we will know what it means to be a *Christian.*

2. Discipleship

Making the first step naturally leads to the second: *discipleship.* We cannot "be Christ" consciously without knowing him. We cannot live his Life authentically unless we walk by his Light. That means opening our minds to the teaching and example of Jesus in the Gospels. It means committing time to the "3R's" of *reading, reflection,* and *response.*

But what makes us able to persevere in discipleship? People constantly make resolutions to pray more, read Scripture, and give time to meditation or group discussions. But sometimes those resolutions don't last very long. What stops us from living up to our commitment to keep learning as disciples?

The first reason is that we haven't really made the first step deeply enough. We are not totally convinced that interaction with Jesus is a necessity, not an extra, in our lives. We haven't despaired enough of everything else to hope all-encompassingly in him. We think we can get along—at least in some areas of our lives—without actively, explicitly, involving Jesus.

Perhaps we haven't accepted Jesus explicitly as an indispensable Teacher, as the Light of the World. We are not fully convinced that the goals and guidance of this world are ultimately "darkness," inadequate to live by. We think we can learn enough from what is available in the culture to live basically happy and productive lives. We don't think we really have to be disciples—students—of Jesus Christ. And so we don't give first priority to learning from Jesus as the Truth, and following him as the Way, in order to be empowered by him as the Life.

Or we may think we have "learned our religion." We may think that through the laws and instruction we have already received we have absorbed the Light of the World. We choose legalism, both doctrinal (simplistic answers) and moral (inflexible rules) over discipleship.

This "dumbs down" the mystery of Christ and Christianity. A mystery is "a truth that invites endless discovery." The infinite truth of God cannot be absorbed completely through any instruction that ends.

But if we study with sufficient "breadth and length and height and depth" (Ephesians 3:18), we will remain at the feet of Jesus, living lives characterized by continuing reflection on his words and example. That is what it means to be a *disciple*.

3. Witness

Then we naturally pass on to the third step. We begin to see how the Gospel applies to life, to see how we can live out the teaching of Jesus in new, creative, innovative ways. We get "prophetic insights" that let us bear witness to the Good News by an eyebrow-raising lifestyle that cannot be explained without it.

That is what it means to be a *prophet*—the first item in our "job description" as the risen body of Jesus on earth, dedicated to continue his messianic mission as Prophet, Priest, and King until he comes again.

But even prophets can fail to act on what they see. Many do. As Jesus himself pointed out, the seed that has broken through the beaten path of culture, that has put down roots through discipleship and has begun to grow, can still be strangled and choked out by "worldly anxiety and the lure of riches" (Mathew 13:22). As we begin to see the radical choices to which the Gospel invites us, we also sense what they will cost. We realize what we may have to give up, what we may lose.

At this point, if we had the support of the whole Christian community, if all the people we are close to were united in making the same radical choices we see we should make, we would go along. There is a sense of safety in numbers. We would rather give up what we enjoy than give up our relationship, our closeness, with others. It is sometimes easier to follow the crowd than to be left behind, even when the crowd is headed for martyrdom.

But the crowd, even the Christian crowd, is always, to some extent, infected by the culture. To be a prophet, then, we have to die to our fear of standing alone. We have to be willing to make radical choices and take frightening risks, even when no one supports us. We have to listen to the Spirit in our hearts and confirm our nonconformity by checking its conformity with the word of God. In more serious choices we consult a spiritual director who can discern with us.

We ask the Holy Spirit for Wisdom and Understanding, for Knowledge and Counsel, the gifts that help us "not be conformed to this world, but transformed by the renewing of our minds, so that we may discern what is the will of God, what is good and acceptable [for Christians] and perfect" (see Isaiah 11:2; Romans 12:2).

And we ask for the gift of Courage, supported by Awe of the Lord, to stand up in prophetic witness to the values of Jesus Christ. And, if necessary, to stand alone.

There are, however, two special dangers to being a prophet.

The danger of pride: To be a prophet is a dangerous thing—not only for the body, but for the soul. When those who have the courage to stand up in solitary witness look around and see they are the only ones standing, they begin to realize they are the only ones who are right—at least about this particular issue. That can lead to pride.

Pride does not mean thinking we are better than others; that is just vanity, an error in judgment. It is not a serious sin. If we are right often enough, we may even conclude that we are smarter than everyone else. There is no sin in that either; it may be the truth!

But if we ever decide that, because we are so smart, then whatever we think must be true, that is the sin of making ourselves the *standard* of truth and falsity. That is pride. Real pride means seeing oneself as the criterion, the standard, of truth and falsity, of good and evil. That is the sin of sins. Only God is the criterion.

Prophets are in danger of getting too wrapped up in themselves, especially when other people react to them. After all, you can hardly be a prophet without attracting notice. People who come out of the desert like John the Baptizer, wearing camel's hair and eating bugs, tend to draw a crowd. They can't even stone you to death without making you the center of attention! That can center you on yourself.

Pride is the first danger inherent in being a prophet.

The danger of alienation: There is a second danger. The crowd that gathers around prophets is often a hostile crowd. Prophets can be threatening. Even if we are not trying to impose our values on anyone, even if all we want to do is live the Gospel authentically ourselves, our example may be a reproach to others. Acts of Christian witness have a way of summoning people to search their own souls. And some don't like it.

So people stone the prophets. Stones hurt. Rejection hurts. Being called wrong when you are right hurts. That can lead the prophet into anger and bitterness.

By the very fact of standing alone, the prophet tends to be alienated from the community. To be different in any way is already in some measure to put oneself on the outside. To be attacked and rejected increases the distance.

So we must not remain just prophets. We mustn't give up being prophets, either, or lessen the radicalness of our prophetic stance. We just have to go further and be *priests.* That means dying to "rugged individualism" in religion, to any attachment we have to keeping our religion an individual affair between ourselves and God, and devoting ourselves to interacting with others in ministry.

4. Ministry

We saw that to be prophets we have to be willing to stand alone. That can degenerate into the corruption of setting ourselves apart from others. As priests we resist that seduction by involving ourselves with others. The faith we express *before* others as prophets we seek to express in union *with* others as priests. We foster relationships. We form community.

In our self-expression as priests, our goal is *relationship.* We interact with others as Christ in order to form relationship with others "in Christ," as members of his body, in the "communion of the Holy Spirit." We give expression to the light, to the love that is within us in order to nurture, to draw people into the life-giving community of redeemed humanity and "promote the whole body's growth in building itself up in love" (see Ephesians 4:16).

To be a priest is to embrace and form community. As "priests in the Priest," we give expression to our faith, hope, and love, hoping to draw everyone together through deep, felt experience of "the grace of our Lord Jesus Christ" and of "the love of the Father," into the "common union" of the Holy Spirit (2Corinthians 13:14). Our focus as priests is on drawing people into the life-giving community of redeemed humanity by bringing about unity and peace, so that "they may all be one" as the Father, Son, and Spirit are one (John 17:21).

It is characteristic of prophets to focus primarily on authenticity, on living out the truth, regardless of consequences. The prophet "lays the ax to the root of the tree" and lets the chips fall where they will. Jesus was speaking of himself as prophet when he said, "Do not think that I have come to bring peace upon the earth. I have come to bring not peace but division. For I have come to set a man against his father, a daughter against her mother, and a daughter-in-law against her mother-in-law" (Luke 12:51).

By contrast, Jesus spoke as priest when he said at the Last Supper, "I pray for the ones you have given me, that they may all be one, as you, Father, are in me and I in you; that they may be one, as we are one; that they may be brought to perfection as one; that the love with which you loved me may be in them, and I in them" (John 17:20).

These two statements are not contradictory. Most of the practical problems in Christianity are solved by thinking in terms of "both-and" rather than "either-or."

Priest and prophet are like oil and vinegar: you need both to make salad dressing. Vinegar alone is too harsh; so is prophetic witness. Oil alone is too bland; so is priestly ministry that does not challenge. Being pure vinegar can alienate one from community. Being pure oil can make one nothing but a facilitator of what the community already wants to do—a pleaser, someone afraid to call for "more." In Jesus the most compassionate, self-giving love the world has ever seen was joined to the most radical challenge the world has ever seen. Jesus was Prophet and Priest.

So we have to be priests as well as prophets. But we must be prophets before we can be priests. If we have never had the courage to stand alone, to take an unpopular stance, to risk arousing hostility in others, how can we know whether our choice to "temper the wind to the shorn lamb" when we moderate our position out of compassion for people's woundedness is really an act of giving priority to love or just a fear of conflict?

5. Stewardship

We can't stop with priesthood. If we did, the Christian community would run the risk of being just a warm, nurturing womb of love, entirely turned in on itself while the world goes to hell in a handbasket.

So we take responsibility for the world, for those around us, for the whole human race. We dedicate ourselves to transforming society, to changing social structures, to working for global peace, to drawing the whole world together in unity under the life-giving reign of Christ.

We have authority from God to do this. This right is ours, as every right is, in virtue of an obligation. We transform society in obedience to the command of him who said, "All authority in heaven and on earth has been given to me. Go, therefore, and make disciples of all nations…." (Matthew 28:18)

By those words we were commissioned as *stewards* of the kingship of Christ, made responsible for extending the reign of Christ over every area and activity of human life on earth.

"All nations" doesn't mean just all geographical entities; it means all areas, all fields of human life and activity. And to "make disciples. . . teaching them to observe all that I have commanded you" doesn't mean just to catechize; it means to instill the attitudes and values taught by Jesus and the policies that follow from these into the social structures and institutions of every culture on earth. It means to renew society, not simplistically or by force, but from within, with respect for the aspirations and goals of the human race created and redeemed by God.

The paradox is that to renew society as stewards of Christ's kingship, we have to abandon our need to see it happen. We have to be willing to persevere in faith and fidelity unconditionally, whether or not we see any results, until Christ comes again, whenever that might be.

Jesus won his victory in the act of accepting defeat on the cross. The supreme triumph of his power was his renunciation of power. He revealed the true nature

of divine power by refusing to triumph except through
human powerlessness. He won life for the world by
accepting death on the cross.

When we are ready to die with him as priests, we will
be ready to conquer the world with him as stewards of his
kingship. To accept that stewardship is the fifth step into the
fullness of the Christian life.

Five Words—One Word

If you want to enter into the fullness of life, go back to
page one of this book and begin reading it again, pausing
as long as is necessary to make decisions as you go.

Better yet, get others to read it with you so that you
can help each other to *understand,* to *decide* and to *act.*
Use the workbook (available through our website, *www.
immersedinchrist.org*).

Jesus came that we might "have life, and have it to the
full" (John 10:10). The fullness of life is yours if you choose
it. Jesus says, "Come, follow me." The way is open, if you
choose to follow it. And the steps you need to take are
clear.

Do you choose to begin?

It only takes one word. It is the word Mary spoke when
invited to be the Mother of God: "Be it done unto me
according to your word" (Luke 1:38). It is the word Jesus
spoke when asked to give his life for the life of the world:
"Father, your will be done" (Luke 22:42).

Five words in one word: "Yes."

FINALE

What am I really proposing—or better, urging—in this book? It is that we choose to make living out these five mysteries our *way of life*.

What is a way of life? It is a sense of identity so strong that it pervades, influences, and gives a special character to everything we do.

Being married can be a way of life if the underlying consciousness of being a spouse or parent has an abiding effect on everything we choose, say, and do; for example, we might not ever buy anything without asking ourselves what our spouse will think about it. Conceivably, a man might be so conscious of being a father that he does not use bad language on the golf course for fear he might use it at home and be a bad example to his children.

Our religion should be a way of life, but frequently it isn't. For many, religion is just a set of doctrines we profess, but do not think to apply consistently, if at all, to

the attitudes and values that determine daily life. We keep
the rules, observe the prescribed practices, and otherwise
live just about like everyone else. Religion can have a very
limited effect on our lifestyle. That is the case when we do
not identify ourselves primarily, before everything else, as
Christians.

But when religion is a way of life, it has a determining
influence on everything we do. It enters into the way we
think, judge, choose, speak, and act—at home, at work,
and at play. It is a mentality, a lens through which we see
the world. All our choices are filtered through it. It is our
identity translated into a lifestyle.

We must grasp and live out our belief that "we have
become Christ" (Saint Augustine's definition of Christians
as quoted above, page 2, and in the Catechism of the
Catholic Church 795). We must proclaim as Paul does, "It
is no longer I [alone] who live, but it is Christ who lives in
me" (Galatians 2:20).

If I am convinced and conscious that the "I" who I am
is not just I alone, but Jesus and I together living as partners
one shared divine-human life in a body that is equally
his and mine, then obviously this will have a determining
effect on everything I think, say, and do. I will be always
conscious that it is not just I who am acting, but that Jesus
is acting with, in, and through me all day long. "It is no
longer I alone who live, but it is Christ who lives in me."
"Being Christ" will become my way of life.

This means, first of all, that I will be aware that by "the
grace of the Lord Jesus Christ" I am sharing in the divine
life of God. I am divine, called to live always on the level of
God. I can only do this, of course, if Jesus is acting *with me,
in me,* and *through* me. That is the first mystery we explained
in this book.

Obviously, if I am going to act in cooperation with
Jesus, I will have to know how he thinks. I will have to

learn from his example. This means I will have to read the Gospels and other parts of the Bible, and do whatever else it takes to learn the mind and heart of God. This means becoming a disciple—that is, a committed student—of Jesus. That is the second element that must be included in my identity as a Christian.

To be Christ, however, necessarily includes taking on the mission of Jesus as Messiah. And I was consecrated to this at Baptism, when the minister anointed me with chrism on the top of my head, speaking the words, "As Christ was anointed Priest, Prophet, and King, so live always as a member of his body." For my way of life to be authentically Christian, I must bear witness as a prophet, minister to others as a priest, and take responsibility for establishing the reign of God on earth as a steward of Christ's kingship. Not to do this is to fail in living an authentic Christian life.

To consciously and consistently live out these five mysteries of Christian identity is what it means to make Christianity a way of life.

Why These Five?

Of all the mysteries of Christianity, why single out these five? Why not focus on Eucharist, or just on living out our Baptism? Or on the *Our Father*, or just on love? Why focus on living out these five mysteries in particular?

The first answer is that nothing else is specific enough. It took Christians centuries to realize it was a sin against love to have slaves. But they would have seen it instantly had they asked if enslaving others was 1) living on the divine level of God, 2) consistent with reflection on the mind and heart of Christ as disciples, 3) bearing prophetic witness to the values of Jesus, 4) giving visible expression to personal faith, hope, and love in ministry to others as

priests, and 5) showing responsibility as stewards of the
kingship of Christ for the establishment of the reign of
God on earth.

The second answer is that these five mysteries are
essential to Christian living. We cannot omit any one of
them and live a complete and authentic Christian life.

Third, all other essentials are inherent in them or cannot
be understood without them.

We do not understand Baptism, for example, unless
we know it gives us five gifts: the gift of divine identity as
Christians, the gift of divine enlightenment as disciples, the
gift of divine empowerment to bear witness as prophets,
the gift of divine surrender and fruitfulness as priests, and
the gift of divine faithfulness as stewards of the kingship of
Christ as we persevere, "hoping against hope," in working
for establishment of his reign. These are all proclaimed in
the rite of Baptism. We just have to pay attention to what
it says.

These five mysteries are the structure of the Eucharistic
celebration, which celebrates them one after another in the
Mass: our new identity in the Introductory Rites, the call
to discipleship in the Liturgy of the Word, acceptance of
mission in the Presentation of the Gifts, surrender to being
priests in the Priest and victims in the Victim during the
Eucharistic Prayer, and a foretaste of the kingdom of God
realized in the wedding banquet of the Lamb during the
Rite of Communion.

We do not fully understand what we are praying for in
the *Our Father* unless we see how the petitions, one after
another, match these five mysteries. "Our Father who
are in heaven" proclaims our divine identity. "Hallowed
be your name" reminds us we must learn God's mind
and heart as disciples in order to make him known and
loved. "Your kingdom come!" expresses acceptance of
our commitment to proclaim the Good News of the

kingdom as prophets. "Your will be done" joins us to
Jesus in his agony in the garden when he surrendered
with these words to being Victim and Priest on the cross.
And the two inseparable petitions, "Give us the bread,"
and "Forgive us as we forgive," are asking for the Bread
of the heavenly wedding banquet which is only given in
a communal meal where all accept each other in total
mutual forgiveness and peace. That is the Kingdom of God
in its fullness.

The seven Sacraments call and enable us to live out
these five mysteries:

Baptism gives us our new identity as Christians.

Reconciliation calls and helps us to keep growing
as disciples. We cannot prepare properly for the Rite
of Reconciliation unless we examine how we are
fulfilling our commitment to live as *Christians, disciples,
prophets, priests,* and *stewards* of the kingship of Christ.

Confirmation empowers us to bear witness as prophets.

Matrimony and Holy Orders commit and empower
us to form community as priests.

The   Sacrament   of   the   Sick   strengthens   our
perseverance as stewards by its promise of ultimate
victory over death.

All of the above is explained and established in four of
the follow-up books to *Reaching Jesus: The Five Promises
of Baptism, Experiencing the Mass, Five Steps to the Father,*
and *Living the Sacraments.* I have also written six books
on Matthew's Gospel that show how Matthew uses these
five mysteries as the outline of his Gospel and develops

each mystery systematically, one after another. All of this just confirms the fact that these five mysteries are basic to Christianity. We find them everywhere.

The Need for a Plan

There is still another question: why do we need a plan? Why not just let the liturgy guide us every year through the mysteries of the life of Christ? Why not just grow into them naturally?

"To fail to plan is to plan to fail." The results show we are failing. Pope Francis felt obliged to "insist on the call to holiness," to urge the whole Church to "devote herself anew to promoting the desire for holiness." He urges us to follow "a path of holiness"—that is a plan—so that the grace of our Baptism will bear fruit (Rejoice and Be Glad, 10, 177, 15). Without a plan good liturgies and good preaching may expose us to everything we need to grow, but our responses will be haphazard, disconnected, and ineffective. A plan makes the difference between formation and just information, between an undefined way of living and a way of life. A plan marks out a path. We always know where we are, where we are coming from, where we are about to go.

The way of life offered here is a plan—not a detailed plan like the religious rule of a third order, not a plan that prescribes certain prayers and actions, but a plan that consists in *systematically focusing* on achieving the five specific *objectives* to which we are committed by Baptism: living as *Christians, disciples, prophets, priests,* and *stewards* of the kingship of Christ.

When we consciously focus, all day, every day, on living out these five mysteries, Christianity, becomes more than a religion, more than a spirituality. It becomes a way of life.

A highway will be there, called the holy way...
It is for those with a journey to make...
(Isaiah 35:8).

If you are one of those with a journey to make, there
is plenty of support for your journey. Go to the website
www.immersedinchrist.org.

For further support of your spiritual growth and
formation, you might try these wonderful books:

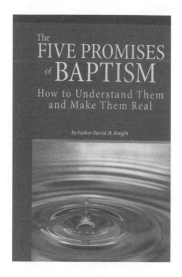

The Five Promises of Baptism
2011 Abbey Press
ISBN 9780870285188

This is an encouraging presentation that reveals the five
mysteries and commitments of Baptism as five promises
God makes to us when we are baptized. It also teaches us
to recognize them as five "ordinary" mystical experiences
inherent in every authentic Christian life. We recommend
it as a follow-up to *Reaching Jesus* and also for R.C.I.A.
candidates and for parents of the newly baptized.

An Everyday Plan
for Following Jesus
With a Preface by Most Rev. Carroll T. Dozier

His Way

1977 St Anthony Messenger;
1997 His Way Communications
ISBN 0942971248

This book is light and humorous in style, challenging and
thought-provoking in content. It has sold over 150,000
copies and been used as a growth tool in several dioceses.
It is a book about knowing and responding to Jesus Christ,
and living our faith in a growing, dynamic way. It gets to the
heart of lay spirituality as a spirituality which focuses, not on
'renunciation," but on union with Christ through involvement
in the world of work and family, social and civic life.

This is the "break shot" book: it breaks open the
topic of personal renewal and Church reform in contrast
to "cultural Catholicism." Typical comment: "Halfway
through, I wanted to throw it across the room." It does
present the five mysteries of Baptism, but without clearly
identifying them. We recommend it as preliminary first
read (to be followed by *Reaching Jesus*) for complacent or
turned-off Christians who are able and ready for challenge.

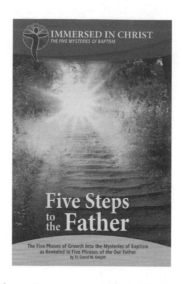

Five Steps to the Father
2011 Abbey Press
ISBN 9780870294655

This book brings the five mysteries and commitments of Baptism into our daily prayer by showing how the petitions of the "Our Father" express and motivate desire to live out each of them in turn. It explains the five steps as five phases of spiritual growth passing through awareness, commitment, dedication, surrender and abandonment. It also explains the seven "gifts of the Holy Spirit" and seven "capital (root) sins" as basic helps and obstacles to spiritual growth. It is an enriched and enriching version of the "roadmap" to spiritual growth. We recommend it as a follow-up to *Reaching Jesus* and *The Five Promises of Baptism*.

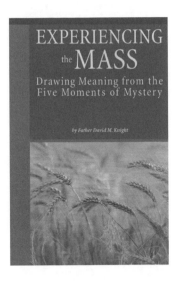

Experiencing the Mass:
Five Moments of Mystery

2011 Abbey Press
ISBN 9780870294525

This book shows how to enter into the mystical experience of Eucharist by showing how in the Mass we celebrate the five mysteries and commitments of Baptism one after another. This enhances our experience of Mass and lets Mass—as "source and summit of the Christian life"—give weekly (or daily) impetus to our forward motion in following the five steps of spiritual growth. We recommend it as a follow-up to *Reaching Jesus* and *The Five Promises of Baptism* and as a stand-alone guide to "full, conscious, active participation" in Eucharist. It is an enlightening book for R.C.I.A. candidates or anyone who is bored at Mass.

Why Jesus? (Book 1 in the Gospel of Matthew Series)

1981 Dimension Books;
1985,1987, 1994, 1997, 1999 His Way Communications
ISBN 0942971019

Matthew's Gospel (believe it or not!) presents each the five mysteries/steps/commitments of *Reaching Jesus* one after another, and develops them systematically. *Why Jesus?* is the first of six books on Matthew's Gospel that show how these mysteries are explained and enriched in the words of God. We predict that anyone who reads *Why Jesus?* will continue with the rest of the series.

Why Jesus? shows us through the first two chapters of Matthew's Gospel what Jesus came to be for us as Savior. It spells out what it means to be a Christian.